Because They Never Asked

A Jewish Family's Search for God

By

Lonnie Lane

D1394396

Dedication

*T*o my cousins – Newt, Rina, Ricky, Dick, Avi, Bobbi, Jessie, Marsha, Kenny and Denny – with whom my brother Michael and I shared all those wonderful Sabbath and holiday dinners while growing up.

Acknowledgements

*A*ny book is a compilation of the input of many into the author's life. This certain is the case with this book. I wish to specifically thank the following dear people for their influence in my life and who helped to make this book possible.

To my Mom, Nesbeth Lane, who is *always* an encouragement, and to my brother Michael who has shared this long journey together with me, and to my sister-in-law Sherry whose love and open heart have always made her home, home to me.

To my faithful 'Tuesday" friends (in alpha order): Wendy Croissette, Sandy Gurin, Pat Kaleta, Dee Parris and Nancy Perot, with ENORMOUS thanks to Nancy Perot for her dedicated editing. And thanks to everyone in "The Gathering" for being behind me in prayer, love and enthusiasm in all my various "missions."

To my friends Nancy Kaplan of *Gates of Prayer Ministries* and to Shantha Edwards of *Shalom Shanthi TV Ministry* (ShalomShanthi.org) for their extraordinarily generous contributions toward making this book a reality. Thanks also to Dick & Bonnie Curtis.

But mostly my gratefulness goes to my Lord, who is Life to me!

Blessings upon you one and all.

Lonnie

Forward

When my Uncle Irv was 86 years old and coming to the end of his life, I went to visit him and Aunt Evie. At a family function several months before, in the course of their conversation, he had told my sister-in-law Sherry that he was reading the Torah. Apparently this was a new experience for him. So it was not surprising that we wound up talking about Judaism and God during my visit. Then he said something to me that I did not expect to hear. "Lonnie," he said, "how could I believe in your God when he took you away from us?"

His question triggered some very deep feelings. Not defensively, but with a longing for connection, I responded gently and respectfully. "Uncle Irv, you're the first person in the family who has even mentioned my beliefs in all these years. Not once has anyone ever asked me how I came to believe in Jesus or why. I know they love me, but no one in the family seemed to want to find out why this was important to me." I asked him to forgive me for my part in any distance there had been between me and the family, which he did.

As I thought about this interaction, I realized how much I really wanted to share this part of my life with my family. I wanted to answer the questions no one had asked and I wanted to bridge the gap that misunderstanding had created.

I wanted to be known by those who had played a major role in my life and contributed to making me the person I have become, each in their own way. This book is an attempt to do just that.

As I wrote, I realized that there were others with whom I wished to share my story as they too were a part of it. Hopefully you will know who you are as you read, though some of you are not directly mentioned in the book. Your real names are not used in several instances to protect your privacy where I thought it would matter to you.

So I offer this book to my cousins in particular, other family members, old friends of my own, and those of my parents' who were like family to me growing up. For those who care to know, here's why and how come, and what happened, not just to me but to my parents, my brother, and for those who knew her and loved her, my mother-in-law.

Lonnie Lane
January, 2004
Jacksonville, Florida

Chapter 1

*T*he speakers on the plane crackled with the announcement I had waited a lifetime for – "Ladies and gentlemen, welcome to Israel."

We burst into applause at the Hebrew-accented announcement, applause that quickly fell into the infectious rhythm played over the cabin PA system to *"Havenu Shalom Alechem."* I longed to join my voice in the song of celebration with the other passengers, but I was too overcome with emotion to utter a sound. Through joyous tears I beheld the Land, green with life, toward which we pressed from the sky. I had but one thought: I had come home!

When at last we had landed, I filed forward with the others, carry-on bags bumping awkwardly over the seat backs, jet-lag weary, yet eager to touch the ground of this sacred homeland. Once outside the plane, I stood at the top of the boarding stairs and inhaled deeply, taking my first breath of Israel. At the same moment, I was struck with both the penetrating heat and an equally penetrating thought, that I was standing at the intersection of my heritage and my destiny.

For a Jew, Israel could never be truly foreign. Once in the airport, I was immersed in the great river of the largest on-going migration in human history – the returning Diaspora. People from many nations, speaking many languages swirled around me. I drank it all in while making sure to stay close to the group of friends with whom we had come. People, familiar with airport procedure, moved purposefully toward Customs. Others were in confusion as they tried to make sense of the signs in Hebrew. Groups looking for their tour guide chattered together in excitement, pointing here and there. Arabs, identifiable by their dress or head coverings, were most likely citizens who had been traveling. But most were Jews, coming home or coming to visit. So many, so different. As different as we Jews were, I marveled at the thought that we were all related, all children of one man, Abraham, who had lived so long ago.

It was March, 1974. I had arrived with nineteen others from our Synagogue, including our Rabbi, Sam and his Israeli wife, Havah, for whom this truly was a home-coming. The specialness and the ordinariness of it all bustled around me – the sounds, the smells, the languages, and the ever-present heat. No air-conditioned airport here. I wanted to inhale it all, greet everyone, see everything, touch everything. This was Israel and I was actually here!

Soon we were through Customs and had boarded the bus on which we would spend much of our days for the next two weeks. As we drove down palm tree lined streets, heading for our hotel, I scanned the signs over the store windows trying to read them with my less than fluent Hebrew. I sounded out the letters on a fairly large brightly colored sign over a store window filled with equally colorful fruits and vegetables. Wondering what it would say in Hebrew, I was somewhat surprised to find it actually said, "Soopr Mahrket."

After a night of trying to sleep off our jet lag, we began our tour. Our guide, Ofir, a pleasant man of about 40, would serve as a walking encyclopedia of the historical significance of each location that we would visit. He proved to have a wealth of stories. To me, Ofir's stories were not about people who lived in this land a long time ago. They were about *my* ancestors, *my* relatives, and this was *my* Land.

In my lifetime, after some 1800 years of being a disen-
franchised people, this very same Land had been restored to
the Jews. The amazing feat of turning uninhabitable malaria
swamps and desert scrub into verdant farmland and forests,
as well as building populated and thriving cities, had all been
accomplished in thirty years. The miracle was evidenced
again and again as the nation introduced Herself to us, one
person, one tree, one productive kibbutz, one sunrise on a
mountain, one sunset in a valley, one potsherd or recovered
ruin and one overcoming accomplishment after another.

We learned that there were Jews speaking 110 different
languages from 86 different nations, streaming into Israel in
fulfillment of the Bible's predictions of the Jews' return to
this same Land after a long absence. I had always been
somewhat proud of the fact that a good part of the world
takes our Bible seriously but I'd never before considered
that it had those kinds of predictive historical facts tucked
into it. To turn all these different people into productive citizens was a massive repatriating effort which involved
teaching each person the language, culture, laws and way of
life in Israel. But it was being done, and the many were
becoming one, they were becoming Israelis.

History is a very present experience in Israel – everywhere we went there was a reminder of some historic event.
Archaeological findings were everywhere, from the time
Abraham first entered Canaan. Events such as when Joshua
conquered Jericho and the walls fell down or when King
David established Jerusalem were clearly evident as were
many of succeeding centuries. I tried to imagine who had set
the worn stones in place on the ancient roadway on which I
now stood. What history had these stones witnessed, I wondered, wishing that they could tell me. Validation of a thriving
Hebrew culture in the Land was as present as the earth itself.
Despite the world's attempt to prove otherwise, one cannot
travel even the shortest distance in Israel without being

confronted with our extensive past in this Land. It was as if the 1,878 years from 70 A.D. when the Romans destroyed the Temple and most of Jerusalem to 1948, when Israel again became a legitimate nation, was a brief hitch in history, albeit a painful one, that took us out of the Land only temporarily.

Havah, grew up in Jerusalem and her mother and Mrs. David Ben Gurion, the wife of the first Prime Minister, hung out their laundry to dry across the alley from each other, talking as housewives always have on laundry day. Havah had arranged for us to visit the Knesset on a day when the re-elected Prime Minister, Golda Meier, was introducing her new cabinet. We sat in an observation gallery behind bullet-proof glass listening to their voices through a sound system as Havah translated the Hebrew into English for us. I was thrilled to see Golda, this tower of a woman whom I revered, as well as Moshe Dayan, Abba Eban, and others whom we recognized. These were the leaders in the new Land for whom I had great respect, some of whom had been leading the country since its birth.

Our visit to the Knesset took place shortly after a school in Kunetra, in northern Israel, had been bombed by the Arabs. Retaliation had occurred in order to stop a further assault. This, of course, was not an isolated incident but the fact that it was a school and that children were harmed made it more shocking in those days before the *Intifada*. Part of Golda's message addressed the Israelis' deep feelings about the latest incident. I have never forgotten what she said as it so embodied Jewish and Israeli values: "We can forgive the Arabs for killing our children," she said in her deep gruff voice, "but how do we forgive them for causing us to kill their children?"

For me, this statement continues to be an example of the true Israeli reluctance in having to retaliate, but having to do so in order to survive. How the world has misinterpreted the Israeli heart. How the media has so misrepresented Israeli intent. My sense of pride in the integrity of my people grew with this and other incidents. At the same time, I also questioned why such hatred continues to exist for the Jews, generation after generation. What did we do to deserve all that suffering?

With regard to suffering, a case in point is what took place on Masada. Masada is a high, flat plateau south of Jerusalem to which the Jews fled in order to escape the Romans after they had destroyed Jerusalem in 70 CE. They set up an entire life style on this huge rock terrace devising ways in which they were able to survive. They managed to hold off the Romans for two years. From the top, you can look down see indentations still evident in the earth of the Roman encampments while they built siege ramps in their determination that these Jews were not going to out-do the Roman army. The Jews were more than equally determined not to violate their relationship with their God by bowing to Caesar as god, nor did they want to be taken as slaves along with their children. They chose instead to commit mass suicide.

As I walked on the top of that plateau among the remains of the homes which these courageous people were somehow able to build with the stones found on or around the plateau, I tried to imagine how they lived their lives while the Romans below hammered and built, intent on their destruction. What did they tell their children the Romans were doing? How did they tell the children that they were all going to die? How do you have the courage to commit such an act? Who does it first? .... How do you say goodbye?

As I considered their plight, it was as if I could hear little tinkling bells around the necks of bleating goats and the laughter of children playing, of adults calling to one another as they went through their activities day by day, for two years. And then I heard … nothing. Silence. As if those 2,000 people were no longer alive. Not one. The experience impacted me as being so real, as if it was happening before me. If I "listen" inside even now, I can still hear the bells and the children … and the silence.

The profound reality of how those people chose death rather than violate the command of God to have "no other gods" before Him moved me deeply. Would I have had that kind of faithfulness to the God of Abraham, Isaac, and Jacob, if I were in a similar situation today? I knew I wouldn't have. I had rarely given God much thought in years. How, I wondered, does one come to the depth of that kind of commitment to a God who, to me, was little more than theory. I pushed away the plaguing thought of valuing God more than one's own life, preferring to stay in the fascination with what they may have lived rather than why they may have chosen to die as they did.

Walking where my very own ancestors may have walked, I wondered if the same rocks or earth I was walking on had once been touched by the feet of a distant grandfather. Could the fragment of a broken clay pitcher I now held in my hands possibly have been created by the hands of my ancestor-grandmother, I pondered, noting that my fingers matched the indentations created so long ago. Who was she? How I wished I could talk with her, know her, understand what her life was like and what hope she felt for her family. How did she relate to being a daughter of Abraham? Did she even think about it? What did it mean to her that she was a Hebrew? The sense of the history of my people surrounded me, like the reality of the wind I can feel but cannot hold.

<<>>

Ofir went along with our curiosity and it was decided that we would venture up to the Golan Heights, an area that had just been taken from the Syrians a few weeks before in the miraculously won 1973 war. The bus bumped its way up narrow winding stone strewn pathways, the front of it often hanging over a cliff, with the wheels inches from the edge. I didn't recall ever having been so frightened. Upon arriving at the top of the Golan we were stopped by armed Israeli soldiers who were quite alarmed that we had made our way up there. "There are mines everywhere!" we were told firmly in Hebrew, confirming the fear of danger that had gnawed at me since we'd crossed the Jordan. We were told with a great sense of urgency to turn the bus around immediately and get back down the mountain without as much as a wheel a centimeter off the dirt road. It took the driver much maneuvering before he got the bus turned around and then he went careening around the bends back down toward the Jordan. I was terrified as I watched our descent out of the front window of the bus heading down the 45 degree angle toward the Jordan River below.

Despite my fear I became aware of a curious scene in front of us. As we descended through the rocky terrain which had been enemy territory three weeks before, the ground was parched and brown with sparse scrub bushes clinging tenaciously only here and there until it reached the meandering ribbon of water which lay below us like a dividing line. On the other side of the river sat a kibbutz, resplendent with lush and green trees. As we drew closer, I could see an abundance of oranges dotting the trees like many polka dots, the trees so heavy with fruit that they could hardly lift their branches to the sun. I was struck with the profound contrast between the landscapes on either side of the river.

As I observed this phenomenon, the words of a Psalm I'd learned as a child in the days when Scriptures were read aloud in schools floated through my mind: *"Thou preparest a table before me in the presence of my enemies.*" Surely here was a bounty of food undoubtedly visible to Israel's enemies only a few weeks before. I had never recalled the Psalm before, not since childhood. Whatever had made me remember that now?

Until that moment I had always considered the Bible to be as the folk tales of my people. I was quite proud to be associated with the writings which much of the world took seriously as wisdom, but I'd never thought of it as being real, that is, really from God. I had believed in God as a child, but God had long ago been relegated to the place of the tooth fairy or Santa Claus. For me God was another childhood story. Though I had loved my Judaism, it was sociological and not theological for me. It was about belonging out of a sense of cultural identity, of being proud of being a Jew for who we are rather than for any belief in God that bound me to my people.

Yet many times I had questioned, if only to myself, whether the survival of the Jews was justification enough in itself. Was there some reason why the Jews continue to survive while other captured, persecuted and scattered peoples had been annihilated or assimilated and had disappeared throughout the centuries? How is it that we have survived? Now, having heard that verse echo through my mind, questions began to form where none had been before. Was it possible that the God of the Bible was still looking out for Israel today?

I kept the thoughts to myself not daring to even ask the question of the others for fear of their answers. Would my friends think I was foolish for even considering the existence of a God who would be concerned for and acting on behalf of Israel's existence? Or did they believe it and would they wonder why this was a new thought to me? Did they take it for granted or would it be a new thought to them as well? Even though we were a Synagogue group, we never talked much about God, I suddenly realized. What did the others think about the existence of the God of Abraham, Isaac and Jacob? What did Sam, our Rabbi, think about the existence of God? I couldn't recall having ever heard him speak about God. Could it be that he had and I missed it? Rather than ask him, I kept my thoughts to myself.

Further fueling the question of Jewish survival was our visit to *Yad Vashem,* the Holocaust Museum. Two things became clear to me as we wandered through the halls that chronicled the unimaginable inhumane plight of European Jews during World War II. Something about Jewish people caused others, even entire nations, to plan to bring about their extinction, while an indomitable spirit remained causing the Jews to have a purpose and a destiny that seemed to be unalterably connected to the national self-image of being God's chosen people.

The holocaust museum experience is an assault to one's sense of all that is humane and is a visual record of the lowest expression of humanity. Though I certainly knew about the *Shoah*, the holocaust, I was not prepared for what I saw. Shocked and overwhelmed by what we witnessed of the cruelty and subhuman plot to extinguish an entire population of people, just because they were Jewish, we asked each other, "Why?" No one had an answer. Had anyone ever had an answer to that question?

Staggering outside of the museum into the heat of the day, I found myself somewhat comforted by the cool serenity and strength of the trees in the Forest of the Righteous Gentiles which surrounds the museum. These trees had been planted in honor of individual Gentiles who had harbored Jews, having risked or given their own lives in order to try and save the lives of Jewish people. In the midst of a society which turned its heads in denial of the mass murder going on around them, these brave people managed to hold onto their compassion and sense of human dignity and chose to value a Jewish life perhaps more than their own. I found some shred of comfort for my alarmed and shaken soul that non-Jews would be so courageous and unselfish as to do that for one of us. Why some and not others, I questioned.

The trees were a salute to each brave hero or heroine who forfeited his or her life in order that a Jew might live, but they also stood proud and strong as a testimony that *Am Israel Chai*, that The People of Israel Live! Even more important, to me these were not impersonal trees – I knew my own grandmother was responsible for at least some of those trees having been planted there.

Chapter 2

When my mother was a child, the Sabbath was a weekly celebration, as it still is in the home of many observant Jews. When she and her four sisters got married, they still came to Sabbath dinners at her parents' house. As their children came along, each one added to the numbers. Some of my earliest recollections of joy are in the home of my maternal grandparents, my most favorite place to be. Often I got to sleep over after the family dinners, spending all of *Sabbath,* that is all day Saturday with "Gramom." It didn't matter what we did together, I just loved being with her. I don't ever remember her telling me she loved me, but love me she did. The only discipline I ever remember her meting out to me was to wag her finger at me, nostrils just a bit flared and say, "Uh, uh, uh, mine kin." That was enough for me. There was nothing that was worth displeasing my grandmother. Even as a teenager that remained true.

Gramom's real name was Yanka, but upon arriving from Russia many years before, she had taken the more American name of Jenny though her thick Yiddish accent would forever keep her identified as a Russian Jew. The same was true for "Grampop" Harry, and while I loved him dearly, it was Gramom that I adored.

Upon entering the house on Friday evening for the Sabbath we would be greeted by the smell of the most delicious dinner imaginable, even though it was the same week after week: chicken soup with matza balls and fresh *challah* (braided bread) to dunk in the soup, a *brust* (brisket), roast chicken with kasha, potatoes doused with onion gravy, and *tzimmis* (carrots and sweet potatoes). For dessert stewed fruit and honey cake. My mouth waters as I write.

At sundown, Gramom would light the *"Shabbas"* candles to welcome the Sabbath. In the winter it would generally mean before dinner. I loved to stand by her as she performed this weekly ritual. With a *schmatah* (cloth) covering her head, she slowly and reverently waved her cupped hands above the flames, beckoning the spirit of Sabbath peace to the household. Her lips moved almost silently in prayer. I was never sure what she was saying as she said it in Yiddish, of which I understood only a very limited amount but I knew as a child only that she was talking with God, and that was cause enough for silent reverence. I stood quietly beside her, awed that my grandmother knew God well enough to have a private prayer with Him, never doubting that He was listening.

The candlesticks were then placed on top of a small china cabinet so that no babies could reach the flames. (Many years later that china cabinet would become a part of my own dining room.) Next to the candlesticks stood a small blue and white metal *tzadakah* box. *Tzadakah* means "gift" or "mercy." It was a bank with a slot in the top for coins and had a picture of three palm trees on it and words in Hebrew. The purpose was to save money to purchase trees in Israel, even before Israel became a State, in order to reclaim the desert in *ha Eretz*, the Land. It was always understood that The Land referred to was Israel. No Jew would ever have had to ask, "What land?"

Gramom faithfully put all her extra coins in the box

each week. Before I reached school age I was sometimes at Gramom's on Thursday's when a very old, or so he looked to me, orthodox Jewish man, would come to the door to collect the coins. He had a long beard and a long black coat topped by a wide-rimmed *frimmel*, a black hat from which hung his *peyes* (long curls) on either side of his head. Peering up at him from my child-height, I never could decide if the side curls came from his hair or were somehow attached to the hat. Despite his kind eyes, I would never have considered asking that question of him, though I always wanted to. He and Gramom would greet each other respectfully the same way every week. He would nod to me with his kind eyes and a smile as I peeked out from behind her skirt. Then he would produce a tiny key which unlocked the little door on the bottom of the *tzadakah* box. The coins would be dumped into a pouch which he then tucked somewhere back into his long black coat. *"Denk you, Zie Gezunt, Meeses Gah-rrelick"* he'd almost chant, rocking a little as he said it. She would respond with *Zie gezunt, rebbe"* ("Good health, Rabbi") and the box would go back on the breakfast room cabinet for another week of coins in order to plant trees in Israel. Never did I think in those days that I would one day find comfort from those trees planted by the coins saved in banks like my grandmothers.

Gramom was the only one in the family who was religious and, therefore, the only one who went to Synagogue. On *Yom Kippor,* my grandfather, my parents, my eight aunts and uncles, seven to ten (depending on who was born or eventually married) cousins, and my brother and I would wait for Gramom to return from a day of fasting in Synagogue to have our traditional holiday meal together. We always came for the *Yom Kippor* break-the-fast dinner of blintzes with sour cream and apple sauce, though no one but Gramom fasted. While we would never have considered abandoning a holiday and not coming together for a meal on the Sabbath or on *Rosh Hashanah* or *Yom Kippor*, and while we always had a *seder* on Passover, no one in the family necessarily took religion seriously. Except, of course, Gramom. Still we were decidedly Jewish. Being Jewish is about identity, it's about culture and it's about values, but not necessarily about going to Synagogue, at least in some circles. One might not even be sure about God, but one thing every Jew is sure about – they are Jewish!

Our music, our food, our writings and our sense of humor, have kept us a people, even though we have been spread all over the world. The binding vision of one day being restored to The Land of Israel has stayed alive in the hearts of Jews the world over for century after century. Each year during the Passover *seder* the words are spoken, "Next year in Jerusalem" to which everyone responds, *Omayn!* (Amen). Each year I heard those words and the story of the Exodus until somehow they became a part of me, as if what had happened to those Hebrews so long ago had somehow happened to me, so that our history was the same. The continuity with my people that I had felt in Israel really began years before at my grandparents' dining room table during Passover.

At one point in my childhood my parents dutifully enrolled me in a Synagogue equivalent of Sunday school. It was not long, however, before I began to ask questions like, "Who did Cain and Abel marry anyway?" to which my teachers had no acceptable answer and I determined, at the young age of eight, that if they didn't even know that, what could they teach me? I told my parents I wasn't going back. Americanized as they were, they didn't seem to care, so that was the end of that. Religion was irrelevant to my parents and consequently to me. Being Jewish, on the other hand, was always relevant. It was what we were. Period.

My mother and all her friends were active members of Hadassah, the Women's Zionist Organization, which educates people about what is happening in Israel as well as about Israel's significance to the Jewish people. It raises funds for the Hadassah Hospital and many other projects on Israel's behalf. One of those projects was and still is Young Judea, which exists for the purpose of teaching Jewish children ages 11-18 about Israel and instilling in them a sense of belonging to Israel. A close friend of my mother's, Rhea Shils, started a Young Judea chapter in our neighborhood which my friends and I greatly enjoyed. Rhea was able to convey to us her own love for Israel as she taught us Hebrew phrases and songs and Israeli folk dances, imparting to us the stories that went behind them. We learned of Jewish pioneers who came from all over the world to help settle the Land and make it a homeland for all Jews everywhere. As we learned of life on kibbutz, it all sounded far more meaningful than anything I'd ever imagined and the nation of Israel became a part of my heart.

As I grew older so did my beloved Grandmother. I became occupied with my friends and eventually no longer spent the Sabbath with Gramom who was no longer able to cook those enormous meals. The magical quality of that day, set apart from the rest of my world, slipped away from me. Despite my reverence for my Grandmother, at some point in my growing-up years I had begun to regard her belief in God as part of her "old country" ways. At the beginning of my teenage years, life being rather difficult for me at that time, I came to the conclusion that if God was really there, life would not be so hard and so many people, including myself, would not be so unhappy.

One particular day I stood for a long time looking out my bedroom window into a gray and empty sky and came to a very grown up conclusion that God simply did not exist. With that conclusion came a feeling of loneliness such as I'd never felt before. I attributed it to the loss of my childhood. I concluded that God had to be put away with other childish things. However, I would spend many years from that day on trying to fill up the emptiness with which that conclusion left me.

Chapter 3

A number of years later, I was married with a son and two daughters. We lived in a beautiful home in a suburb of Philadelphia which at that time was still somewhat rural. The old farmhouse had a big stone barn and several acres of pastureland. At this point, my life was pretty much occupied with my husband and children as well as riding our several horses and playing tennis. Life was good. Being Jewish wasn't in the forefront of our lives. Both Gramom and Grampop had passed away. The family continued to have our large dinners but only on holidays now though we maintained our yearly Hanukkah party with the plethora of gifts for everyone. I always loved when we came together. For my husband and myself, though, Judaism was not particularly relevant to our lives. Not that we would have ever denied it but the topic rarely came up outside the extended family.

Our lives took a different turn, however, the day that my six-year old son, Ricky, came home from school in his first week in kindergarten crying and frightened. I gathered him into my arms trying to calm him enough to find out what happened. "Some kid told me I was a Christ killer," he said, sobbing in my arms. "I never killed anybody. And I don't even know anybody with that name." Alarmed that this would come up in my life of perceived safety, those words coming from my frightened son brought a realization that our Jewishness was in fact very relevant. How was I to protect him from that kind of ignorance? We decided that if he was going to be identified as a Jew he might as well know what being a Jew was all about. Soon after we joined a Synagogue.

While it is not necessarily true that all who belong to Synagogues believe in God, somewhere along the way I had come to believe again in God, although not the classical Judaic view of God, (whatever that was.) It had been a long journey from the day when as a young girl I had decided that God was a childhood fable. When my husband entered law school at the University of Pennsylvania the people that we met opened up to us a wealth of new ideas and concepts. One of those was that God, in whatever form that may be, did exist.

I had become friendly with one of the other law school wives who was the smartest woman I had ever met. Talking with her was stimulating and exciting. When she had some spiritual experiences that were entirely new to me – and to her – I trusted that anyone with an I.Q. like hers was likely to have found some truth. Later I would decide that intelligence does not necessarily mean wisdom when not coupled with discernment. In other words, smart does not always mean wise. I eventually learned there are good and bad spiritual influences. I soon ended my relationship with this woman, unwilling to go where she was going. However, those experiences brought me to the realization that a spiritual world exists around us and affects our lives. Life was not just humanity and chemistry existing in an evolutionary pond without meaning.

In contrast to this woman was one of my husband's law

school buddies. He was an example of integrity to me as I watched him struggle with issues of honor and uprightness others might not have considered in the same way. While I had come to an openness concerning the reality of a spiritual dimension, that did not mean "God" by any means. I couldn't believe that any thinking person would actually hold to the concept of a knowable and interactive God who cared about his creation, let alone them personally. At that time the popular existential, philosophical opinion about God was that "God is dead." But when this man of intellect, tenderness and character firmly stated in more than one conversation on the subject that he firmly believed in God, it impacted me greatly. In time, though I doubt that he was at all aware that he had projected this to me, his unwillingness to do what might offend his God and adversely affect his relationship with Him, though he mentioned it only once, brought me across a vast chasm toward accepting the existence of a moral God.

Once we became members of the Synagogue, all that I had learned in the Young Judea group blossomed in my heart. Because I am a natural joiner, it didn't take us long to become involved. The holidays had always been special to me, but attending holiday services deepened their meaning to me. I began baking a large *chalah* (braided bread) on Fridays for Sabbath and lit my own candles saying the same prayer my Grandmother had said when I had stood so quietly by her side. Our Sabbath dinners at home were followed by our attending services at the Synagogue each Friday night. I particularly loved the special occasions in Synagogue, or an O*neg Shabbat* which is a social time following the formal service where refreshments are served. Sometimes it included singing and dancing to lively Israeli

29

music. The music wrapped itself around my soul and my sense of pride and belonging as a Jew, and our connection with Israel swelled within my heart.

There was a particularly strong awareness in the Synagogue kitchen of continuity with Jewish women spanning centuries and continents, when together with other women we made chicken soup for *Pesach* (Passover) or baked *Humentashen* (pastries shaped like Haman's hat) for the *Purim* party which centers around the Book of Esther in the Bible. I loved participating in the observant Jewish community, even though it was Reform and not the orthodox Judaism of my Grandmother.

The Synagogue became the center of our social life. We developed a group of friends which included Rabbi Sam and his wife Havah and others, most of whom were on the board of the Synagogue so often our discussions were Synagogue or Judaism related. As a group we shared dinners, movies, and skiing. We had Passover seders together which, when at Sam and Havah's, went on till midnight – the real thing, the whole *megilla* (story). We also went to Israel together, along with other Synagogue members on that memorable trip.

After returning from the trip to Israel, I found that certain questions had followed me home. No matter how much I tried to dispel them, they remained like the aroma of bread that lingers way after it is taken from the oven and put away for later, leaving you hungry for some now. The questions came from a series of experiences I had had in Israel. They seemed to have a theme about them which clung to my mind and wouldn't let go, in spite of my wish that they would.

Not only was I perplexed about the Psalm that had gone through my mind while coming down from the Golan Heights, and the questions about the continued persecution and yet the survival of the Jewish people – *Dayenu* – that would have been enough already. But while there I had sensed the perplexing presence of one particular Jewish Rabbi of old in who's name great sorrow and misfortune has befallen the Jews. While in Israel I repeatedly had had an awareness of the man called Jesus. What in the world was I to do with this? I hadn't planned to think about him. I didn't even want to think about him. But the thoughts persisted. I just wanted them to go away. It seemed like he was following me around, just out of sight but there nonetheless. I tried to dismiss the thoughts but they took up residence in my mind.

After several months, I decided to try talking with Sam about Jesus. I mean, after all, who talks to their Rabbi about Jesus? I summoned up my courage and as casually as I could manage, one day I finally asked Sam, "How come we Jews write down the thoughts and interpretations of Scripture from every Rabbi for centuries but this Jesus, who was acknowledged as a Rabbi, is shunned like someone unclean? If he was a Rabbi why is there such antagonism toward him?"

While we discussed it as a somewhat interesting intellectual topic for a short while, Sam had nothing satisfying to say on the subject that would put my questions to rest and I continued to wonder what power there was about this man that his name evoked such reaction from the Jewish people. Perhaps it was, and justifiably so, because of all that has been done to us Jews over the centuries in his name, such as the Crusades, the Spanish Inquisition and the atrocities perpetrated by Nazi Germany, to name a few. Would Jesus, himself a Jew, have led such horrible persecutions against his own people? Was what came about historically in this man's name representative of him personally, or was he misrepresented to the Jews the way we Jews have been misrepresented to the rest of the world, I wondered. Could it be that who he really was has been so distorted that he has been made out to be an enemy of his own Jewish people, which he never intended?

I had other nagging thoughts for which I could find no satisfactory answers. My mind went round and round with a seemingly unanswerable question: How can we possibly come to know an infinite God with our finite minds? At the same time I wondered why people long to be loved unconditionally when it is so rare. The closest I had seen unconditional love was the way my Gramom loved me, but I knew that even that wasn't entirely unconditional. And if it is non-existent, why do we all long for what doesn't exist? Why would we seem to have a need, each one of us, for what is non-existent? I never connected my questions about Jesus with these questions.

One day Havah and I were having a discussion about God, which I probably had started. "Sam considers God to be an abstract possibility," she said pensively. A Rabbi himself, I thought, and he had no more answers than I had. He seemed to be at peace with it, however, though I was not. I envied what appeared to be the orderliness of his assessment of it all. Sam had been raised as an orthodox Jew, though he had found no satisfaction for his astute intellectual mind in the strict adherence to Rabbinic law and so he had left the orthodox community. Yet he strayed only far enough to become a Rabbi in a Reform setting.

"How come King David could hear from God and we can't," I asked Sam earnestly one day. It was yet another question that often tugged at my mind, begging for an answer. "Why could the prophets of Israel hear God's voice and we can't today," I questioned. No one I knew ever heard God's voice. Did Sam? Did anyone he knew? Sam began to wonder himself, not about my questions but about the soundness of my mind in asking all these questions.

"Lonnie," he said leveling a look into my eyes so I would be sure to hear what he was saying. "It's one thing for us to talk to God, but it's *meshumed* (crazy) to think that we could hear from God." He suggested that I consider seeing a psychologist about my inordinate preoccupation with such questions about God.

I decided, instead, to take a graduate course in comparative religions at the Temple University campus nearby to get some answers. I immersed myself in reading about the great religions of the world, including Judaism, as well as Christianity, with its supposed Jewish roots. I became fascinated with the extent of the Hebraic foundation of Christianity. Yet with all the knowledge I found that I had no more answers that satisfied me than my Sunday school teachers had given me long ago. I was always learning but never coming to a knowledge of the truth, it seemed. Objective truth was what I longed for.

Ever since my teenage years I had been looking for truth, hoping that I would recognize it when I came upon it. So far it hadn't happened. Now none of the philosophies I was studying provided the "Aha!" that I was looking for either. I began to question whether there something wrong with me that I was even looking for something called 'Truth'. Was there really no such thing as objective truth? Was it non-existent, like unconditional love? Are we left only with the searching but never the resolution to our dilemma? If that was the case I saw nothing ahead but despair. Was I destined to try and keep myself occupied with something, only to have to find the next supposedly meaningful thing when that wore off? Wasn't there anything ultimate? Fully purposeful? Was it to be found in Judaism? And if not, why bother to maintain our Judaism against such antagonism as exists? Was the only justification for being Jewish that we had always been Jewish and so we should continue to be. Was that reason enough?

Chapter 4

*J*ust when I was beginning to think that Sam might be right, and I was doubting my own soundness of mind, I met a sweet and gentle woman who changed the way I thought about it all. I had been a medical technician before I was married. It came into my mind one day that I should keep my hand in my medical technology skills and look for a job. I thought about it for a day or two and when I'd gotten as far as wondering where I would begin to look for a job, Suburban General Hospital popped into my head. Not that I needed a job or something else to do, with three kids and a husband, taking a few courses at the college, and my involvement with the Synagogue. By this time I had given up the horses as they required more time and attention than I was now able to give them since going to school. I did still keep my weekly tennis game. Even with all that to do, I felt suddenly drawn to working in a hospital again. Following this unction, I walked into the personnel department of the hospital and asked about a possible job as a med tech. "I suppose you're answering the ad in the paper," said the woman behind the desk. I hadn't known there was one, but OK, I'd be the answer to the ad.

I got the job, and had been working for several weeks when a woman named Nancy Perot came to work in the lab. The first day she arrived, while I was out on the floor with the patients, I happened to walk past the time clock of the hospital and saw a woman punching in. Now there are several thousand people working in that hospital at any given time and I surely didn't know them all, but it seemed the most natural thing in the world that I recognized this stranger as the new woman coming to work in the lab. I approached her and found out that's who she was. I introduced myself and offered to show her to the lab and my friendship with Nancy began.

One day at lunch in the hospital cafeteria several of us were talking about a certain patient who had just died after having been hospitalized for long enough for each of us to know her. I mused out loud, "I wonder who she's going to be in her next life." For all my cultural Jewishness, I had read enough comparative religious material so that somewhere along the line I had decided that reincarnation sounded like a more plausible explanation than nothing at all after death. Nancy, who was a soft spoken, rather shy young woman immediately answered, "Oh no. People die only once and then stand judgment, the Bible says." I looked at her in surprise. "And where do you expect to go when you die?" I asked, sure that I knew and she didn't. With uncharacteristic assurance Nancy replied, "I'm going to heaven to be with Jesus."

Her answer almost amused me. Isn't that cute, I thought. I didn't know people still thought that way. It seemed naïve and foolish to me. After all, I was a student of religions, many of which supported reincarnation. To heaven to be with Jesus indeed! I had to admit that I was impressed with the strength of Nancy's conviction that it was true, at least to her. It was nice for her that it was a comfort to her even though it was completely unfounded. No matter. We'd all go on from life to life anyway as far as I was concerned, even if I'd never heard it mentioned in Synagogue. Nancy and I would chat about religion from time to time.

<<>>

One day Nancy brought a book to me. "Here, this is for you. I thought you'd like to read it," she said as she handed it to me. It was entitled *The God Who Is There* by Francis Schaeffer. I took the book home and was not far into it before I realized that this book somehow answered one after another of the questions I had entertained for years as well as those that had formed in my mind since encountering the Rabbi named Jesus in Israel. I had read books about Christianity for school before but that had been theoretical and was juxtaposed with other religions ("This religion believes this, while that one believes that") Schaeffer, however, wrote with a conviction that what he was saying was entirely valid as the only way to see things correctly. On one hand I felt like I was eating *traif* (unkosher foods) reading this Christian stuff, but on the other hand, it was making sense to me as few things had before. Despite my trepidation, I continued to read.

As an artist myself I had wondered how art had made the journey from realism to abstract and to minimalism. What philosophical change had occurred that made what would have once been seen as wholly unacceptable as art now valued as art with deep meaning? And what was the significance of the change? I had often felt that I'd missed something since I'd never gotten it, whatever it was. Schaeffer talked about the trend away from traditional religious values and lives that had been firmly anchored in God and the Bible as was happening in our society thereby causing a growing sense of lawlessness and a certain element of chaos, which are reflected in both modern art and music.

This "chaos" was familiar to me. The Rabbis identify the world we live in ever since Eve ate the apple as the age of chaos. It is supposedly the expected Messiah who is to come and bring an end to the chaos and restore the universe to God's original order. Without God and without Messiah, the world continues in moral chaos, according to Jewish thought. Modern art and music, Schaeffer said, being philosophically birthed, are expressions of the increasing moral decay as people and society grow further and further from personal relationships with God. His premise was that without God and without a reliance on the truth in the Bible upon which the Judeo-Christian values of our country were founded, such values change like shifting sands or clouds blown by the wind. Objectivity is lost to subjectivity. It amounts to what happened during the period of the Judges described in the *Tenach* (Old Testament) when "everyone did what seemed right in their own eyes."

If that was the case, wasn't anybody in charge? How many times I'd worried about just that – no one seemed to be in charge. I'd come through the 60's and we were now in the 70's. Enough had happened that in my estimation we humans were capable of destroying not only ourselves but the world as we knew it. "If it feels good, do it," had been the credo for a while. Where was the stability in that? Is there anyone really in control? It had never occurred to me that God might be, at least not until I read *The God Who Is There*.

For the first time, I could see how losing my sense of God had left me without an anchor to real values. It was truth that I sought to find – in the poetry I read or wrote in my attempts at wordsmithing, or in my art as I tried to pull reality into shape with clay or force it to come forth with a brush and color. For the first time I saw that a society that dismisses God as well as the Bible upon which our values as both Jews and Christians were founded, is a society that loses its mooring. This was a great deal to be thinking about.

The next morning, I greeted Nancy with a question as soon as I saw her at the lab. "How did you come to pick out this book for me? What made you buy this very one?" I asked. There are thousands of books in any bookstore – was it a coincidence that she managed to select a book that answered so many of my questions? "The Lord told me which one," she answered in her gentle matter-of fact tone, as if this wasn't the most important answer I had ever received. I was astounded at her reply. "He talks to you? God talks to you?" I asked incredulously. "Yes, I asked him which book and he told me this one." My Rabbi didn't hear from God, no one else I ever knew heard from God, but Nancy hears from God! That's when I asked if we could meet to talk. I needed to know more.

Over a cup of coffee in the hospital cafeteria, amidst the clatter of dishes and the din of voices, Nancy explained, "Our sins are what separate us from God. When we're separated from God we can't hear his voice." This kind of talk was all new to me. First of all, I was a nice Jewish girl. I didn't have any sins, of that I was pretty sure. But I did know I didn't ever hear God's voice. Was my deciding God didn't exist when I was eleven a sin? Did that cut me off from hearing his voice? Does he speak but I can't hear him? Or isn't he talking to me anyway? Then again, why would God want to speak to me? And what would he say if he did. I couldn't imagine.

"But Jesus died to pay the price for our sins," Nancy continued, "so that they are no longer counted against us by God because of what Jesus did. He took the punishment that our sins deserve. When we accept that for ourselves, then we are no longer separated from God and we can hear his voice."

Astounding, I thought, that Nancy or others would believe such a story. It seemed preposterous to me. The idea of sin was completely foreign to me. I keep all the commandments, I told myself, not that I could have told anyone what they all were. Our coffee break came to an end and I paid for my coffee wishing I could just as easily pay for all this to go away and not bother me anymore. But the persistent questions in my mind had stirred up the soil of my soul into which the seeds of Nancy's assurance fell and began to take root despite my attempts to dismiss the whole thing.

As a sculptor I often found inspiration and at times solace in the Rodin Museum. Rodin was the first sculptor to divert from the classical style of the Greeks to produce what was considered sculpture with more of a psychological than a classical emphasis. His pieces didn't just stand there looking like Greek statues. They drew you in. They told you what the subjects were thinking about or what they were engaged in. Consider for instance, his well known piece entitled, "The Thinker" with which most of us are familiar. You know he's thinking. You almost feel like you're invading his privacy as you watch him think.

One particular life sized piece was of a man walking quite purposefully, which is so realistic that Rodin was accused of casting it from a human model rather than sculpting it. That piece was his John the Baptist. John walks with determination, as if he knows exactly where he's going and why. The one remnant of classical sculpture is his right hand, palm open toward his chest and held at chest height, fingers slightly curled, with his index finger pointing toward heaven. This pointing finger was always a clue that that person, whether in a sculpting or painting, was a person of religious significance.

One day, I took my questioning mind to the museum, hoping for some quiet meditative solace in the peace of the museum. Just being in the presence of the genius of Rodin was soothing to my soul. I came upon John the Baptist, who was as before still standing in mid-stride, with all his determination to accomplish his task. All I knew about John was that he was the precursor to Jesus, and that he had announced Jesus' coming to the Jews who came to him on the banks of the Jordan River.

I was alone in that section of the museum on that particular afternoon. As I stood and looked at him anew, wondering about this John the Baptist person, I wished that he could talk and tell me what his message was. What was it that had taken place among those Hebrews then that no Jew that I knew would even touch today? Then, as if drawn to John, I slowly slid my hand into his, the hand which pointed toward heaven. I was surprised that mine fit so easily and properly into his, as if his cool bronze hand welcomed my own. I was holding hands with John the Baptist! From deep within I whispered, "Take me to the one you know." I stood there in the power of that moment, then withdrew my hand, and quietly – pensively – I left the museum.

Chapter 5

I began to ask more and more questions of Nancy which she was unable to answer. She had, after all, only become a Christian several months before while watching the 700 Club on TV. She suggested that I meet with a woman named Maxine with whom she had been doing some Bible studies. I was ready for Maxine to come the next day but she wouldn't agree to come for two weeks. On the day that Nancy brought Maxine to my house, I had baked some chocolate chip cookies in anticipation of a nice chat over tea. Maxine arrived in a flurry of purposeful activity. At the barest introduction she opened her large attaché case out of which she took a concordance and a large Bible. She tossed several tracts on the table with such titles as "How a Rabbi Found Peace."

Maxine began to tell me that I was a sinner and that I could have forgiveness and eternal life through Jesus. Here was that sinner business again. I knew that didn't apply to me, first of all, and secondly, my eclectic Judaism included the assurance that I already had eternal life through a succession of reincarnated lifetimes to which somehow God, whoever he was, gave oversight. I wasn't impressed.

She continued to tell me that there were thousands of Jews in Israel and around the world who had come to believe that Jesus was the Messiah in fulfillment of prophesy, and that he was returning to earth again to reign and rule as God. While I'm sure it was well thought out to Maxine, it made little sense to me. Within an hour of her arrival, she tossed her books back in her attaché case without having opened them, left the tracts on the table and was out the door without, I might add, eating even one of my chocolate chip cookies. Climbing into her big VW van, over her shoulder she called out, "If you want to know more, give me a call," and with a roar of exhaust she barreled out the driveway and was gone.

Well, I wanted no more, I was sure of that. I threw the tracts away and purposed to put the entire Jesus thing behind me once and for all. But days later, after reading the tracts after all, I called Maxine when I still couldn't get this Jesus to go away. "Find me someone Jewish to hear this from," I requested. Even if it's remotely true, I thought, I need to hear if from someone Jewish. Within an hour Maxine called me back and said as if arranging a clandestine appointment in a mystery novel, "Meet me in the parking lot of the Sheraton Hotel on Thursday at three o'clock," then she hung up. What was I doing, I asked myself. This is crazy. Yet three days later I met Maxine at the Sheraton, and got into her VW bus to drive to the home of a woman named Marlene Rosenthal.

A half hour later we arrived at a small Levittown tract house which looked precisely like every other house on the block. We knocked on the door which was opened by Marlene who was a pleasant looking dark haired woman in her 40's or so, who greeted us warmly; she had been waiting for us. One significant thing caught my attention immediately: Around her neck she was wearing a Star of David, but this one had a cross in the center of it. My whole life those two symbols were anathema to one another, and she was wearing them as if she expected that they belonged together. Already I was nervous but her warm hospitality soon made me feel more relaxed. She had even made homemade pretzels.

We sat down at her kitchen table and began to talk. Getting right to the point, Marlene opened the Bible that was sitting on the kitchen table as if it always lived there, available when wanted, and began to show me Old Testament prophesies of the coming Messiah and their New Testament fulfillment in Jesus. Despite my involvement in Synagogue, I had little knowledge of what was actually in the *Tenach*. While I had often heard a Yiddish expression from my paternal grandfather that this or that would happen "*ven da Moshiah cumin,*" that a Messiah would actually come was an alien concept to me. I had no idea that there were predictions in our Hebrew Bible that would enable us to recognize the Messiah should he actually come on the scene. In fact, I had little knowledge of the Bible at all. It had never been an issue before. Some Talmud, yes. Some do's and don'ts, some wisdom. But to Marlene, there was only one book of authority and it was the Bible. I was impressed with the expertise and familiarity with which she flipped back and forth between the *Tenach* and the New Testament, but it seemed to me as if she was trying to put round theological pegs into square holes.

There was nothing antagonistic or "I know better than you" in Marlene's tone. Nothing put me on the defensive, as I had expected. Yet it was making little sense to me. As politely as I could manage it, I said, "If you're telling me that some man died on a cross 2000 years ago and somehow that has the effect of eliminating sins I don't even believe I have so that I would then be acceptable to God, it makes no sense to me. And besides I'm a Zionist through and through. I could never give up being Jewish." This was obviously not working, I told myself.

One by one Marlene, not the least bit intimidated by my not believing what she was telling me, began to answer my objections. I had known that Yeshua was Jewish but I didn't know that all the apostles, including Paul were also Jewish.

Somehow I had missed that fact. She told me that the New Covenant or Testament, just like the Old Testament, is a Jewish book written by Jews to Jews. Well, that put a new spin on it for me. "You're saying the New Testament is Jewish, not Gentile?" I asked incredulously, wondering why this was new information to me. Yet, true to my Talmudic heritage I continued to debate the issues, hoping for a resolution to the perplexing dilemma before me as to why I was even there in the first place asking about Jesus. For all I'd been through – with Nancy, with God telling her to give me the *God Who is There* book, with John the Baptist – that I was in the throes of dealing with Jesus was still perplexing and foreign to my Jewish mind and heart.

As for being a sinner, while I did know that repentance was a wholly Jewish concept – that is after all what *Yom Kippor* is all about – I was still quite sure I wasn't included in the company of those who might be considered sinners. While I knew people whom I might put in that category, I certainly didn't see myself as one of them. Marlene apparently saw it differently but didn't push the issue. "It will take the *Ruach haKodesh,* the Holy Spirit of God, inside of you, to teach you about that, to teach you what holy and unholy is," she said calmly. How could I argue with that? I didn't even know what it meant to have the Holy Spirit inside of me. I assumed that she thought this would be a good thing. She obviously had some information to which I was not privy.

"We have all violated God's commands to be holy as He is holy," Marlene said as if she was hearing my own dialogue with myself. Who can be holy like God, I had asked myself, not sure that I even remotely knew what holy was. I may not be a sinner, but whatever it is, holy I'm not. Maybe that's the point, I silently agreed to myself. Jesus said, 'You must be born again,'" Marlene continued. "When we appropriate his death as His having taken our punishment for our violation of God's Commandments, no longer do our sins separate us from God. The Holy Spirit then comes into our hearts and we are made newly alive to God Who is Spirit, as if we were born anew, starting life all over again from an entirely new perspective – with God.

This sounded familiar – Nancy had told me the same thing. But it was still just information to me, not truth. It still sounded like *nahdishkeit* (foolishness) to me. A sense of futility stole over me as I struggled to have it make sense, yet not sure that I really wanted it to make sense.

What happened in the next few moments was the single most extraordinary and yet the most natural thing that has ever happened to me in my entire life. In the time that it takes to say one two-syllable word, everything changed. As I struggled with what Marlene was saying to me, I suddenly heard a voice, a very male voice, as if a man had leaned down behind me and had spoken into my right ear. I heard it as audibly as I was hearing Marlene's voice, but neither Marlene nor Maxine gave any indication of having heard it.

While none of this was conscious at that moment, I would later observe that The Voice carried with it a profound sense of the Person of the Speaker. The Voice conveyed to me His unchallengeable authority and at the same time His capacity to bring about a deep and comforting peace that was beyond anything I'd ever known in my life.

The word He spoke to me had been "Listen." I didn't think about it or decide to heed it. I didn't even make the observation that it was the Voice of God that I had just heard. It just was and I just listened. Like when God had said, "Let there be light" and light was. God had apparently said "Listen" to me and so without striving to be or to know or to do, I just – listened.

Marlene and Maxine were oblivious to what had just taken place. All they knew was that I was no longer arguing my points. Maxine, as if on cue, decided that we'd done enough talking and wanting to cut to the real issue at hand she said, "Do you want to pray and accept Jesus as your Messiah?" Even then I still wasn't sure what it all meant and as for praying, I didn't know how to pray except to repeat the prayers in the *Sidur* (prayer book) in Synagogue. But after what I'd just heard I had the overwhelming sense that this was what I had been searching for for years, and to walk away from this was to be sorry that I had done so for the rest of my life. Maybe even longer, the thought occurred to me. Even though I'd heard His Voice, I knew that I still had the freedom to choose. After a moment I chose to say yes to Marlene's offer to lead me in prayer.

I took the hands that were offered to me as the three of us sat at the kitchen table and began to pray. "God of Abraham, Isaac and Jacob," Marlene began. "Thank you for Lonnie." She's thanking God for me, I wondered. "Lord, she's asking to know if Yeshua is her Messiah. Grant that she may fully come to know you with assurance in her heart," she prayed. Then turning to me she began to lead me in the words of a prayer. Despite my discomfort with the newness of this experience, I repeated after her.

"Dear Lord.... I do not fully understand all this.... But I ask you to show me the truth of it.... Please forgive me for my sins, whatever they might be....and come into my life....and teach me how to live for God.... I thank you that Jesus died for me so I would not have to be separated from you any longer...because he took the penalty of my sins for me....I thank you for giving me eternal life...and that I can know that I am going to heaven to be with you forever when I die....I pray this in Jesus' name, Amen."

When I lifted my head from praying that simple prayer tears were streaming down my face, much to my embarrassment. As we had prayed, it had felt as if chains were snapping inside of me, being broken and I was being set free.

Free from what, I wouldn't know for a while, but I knew that something very significant had taken place. I knew I had had an encounter with the God of Abraham, Isaac and Jacob. I also knew without a doubt that this Jesus was the Messiah that my people had been waiting for. With that one prayer, God had transported me from one place to another, from a mindset of confusion to one of assurance. Suddenly I understood what had been hidden from me moments before. What I couldn't comprehend with my mind, God had done by his Spirit. While I didn't understand much more than that, I knew that it was the truth. I had finally found Truth and of all places I had found it in Jesus. With it came a peace that enveloped me – it was unlike anything I had never known.

Marlene and Maxine were overcome with delight and joy. While I knew that I had had a wonderful experience, their jubilation surprised me. The fact that they kept thanking God for this further surprised me. Never mind. I assumed that it would eventually become clear to me I really was, it appeared, born again!

That took place on the day before my birthday. All my birthday cards that year said, "Congratulations on the day of your birth." The sun shone brightly, the flowers were brighter, and the depression that had enveloped me for so very long was gone. Just two weeks before I had walked past a mirror and caught a glimpse of myself and I was shocked by how old and downcast I had looked for my age, as if life had disappointed me greatly. My eyes had seemed dull and dark and it had frightened me when I saw it. The day after my born-again experience I happened to walk past the same mirror and, catching another glimpse of myself I was again shocked, this time by seeing how alive I looked, like a woman with an entirely different countenance. I saw a light in my eyes that expressed what I felt in my heart and it was Jesus!

Days later, as I replayed that Voice in my mind over and over again as I would continue to do for many years, I pondered what I had heard in that one word, conveyed not by the word but by the Voice. No human being ever spoke with the sovereign authority inherent in the Voice or such complete tenderness, and surely not simultaneously, as if within the Owner of this Voice these were mutually inclusive, as if power and compassion were complimentary, one to bring about the other.

I would from then on describe hearing the voice of God as the single most natural moment of my life, as if all else in life is like walking in waist-high water through which you have to push to move forward. This was a moment of complete and entire freedom from any striving or effort and peace without hindrance. It came with the conviction that this was how life is meant to be, at one with our God in His peace.

One day it struck me that I had actually heard the same voice of God that Abraham had heard when God told him to leave his father's household and head toward a Land He would show him and I had heard the same voice that Moses had heard at the burning bush when God told him to go back to Egypt to set His people free. This was the same voice that Moses heard on that on-fire, smoking, *shofar*-blasting mountain when God gave him the Ten Commandments. I had heard that same Voice of God! The only Voice of God. Over and over I would "re-listen" in my head, to remember how it sounded, awed by the reality that God Himself had spoken to me. All those questions as to why God no longer speaks, and now God had spoken to me!

I understood now why those who heard His voice went when God told them, "Go." It would be as incomprehensible to deny the One to whom that Voice belongs as it would have been for light to decline to "be" when He said, "Let there be light," or for a lover, longing for her loved one, to turn away at the sound of his voice rather than run to him.

I also realized that for the first time my Judaism made complete sense. It wasn't just about us as Jews, it was about the redemption of the entire world, beginning with the children of Abraham. God was the goal and relationship with Him was offered to all who would come to Him. It was not just the preservation of one people group. There was much to learn and I knew I was only at the beginning of a life-time of being taught by God. I also knew, as a Jew, the portrayal of Jesus as the Gentile-God was incorrect and somehow God had to correct this. I was delighted to learn that His real name in Hebrew is not Jesus, but Yeshua, a name close to Joshua that means "God is Salvation" or "God saves." While the concept of salvation was foreign to me, I knew that He had indeed saved me. He became "Yeshua" to me from then on.

Within a few days of praying to accept Yeshua into my life I realized that something had already changed – me! Life felt different. Gone were the continual obsessive questions. I felt somehow whole, as if a place inside that had always been lonely and empty was now filled. Life itself, in a short period of time, began to take on a whole new meaning and depth. From that day when I prayed with Marlene and Maxine God had begun to occupy my thoughts. I was fascinated with an extraordinary Someone. I was seeing life from a different perspective, His perspective, as much as I knew of it at least. I found myself desiring to be with God, to talk to Him, to just be in His presence, which amazingly enough was as close as turning my thought to Him. Having Him in my life wasn't a matter of coming to some philosophical or religious belief. It wasn't like deciding to become a Republican when you'd been a Democrat all your adult life, or join an association or movement of which you were now a member. I had met God in the Person of Yeshua. He was not just an historical figure but I was finding that He was very much alive and present with me. It was more like I had met Someone and I had fallen in love with Him and loved being with Him. It wasn't a set of ideas. He was *with* me. His presence was very real to me and it satisfied something inside of me that had been entirely untouched before.

With Yeshua in my life, what had been an unidentified longing turned into contentment. A void had been filled with my new relationship with God! However He had done it, I knew this was real and was the most life-changing experience that I had ever had. During my busy days I'd go to my bedroom and kneel by my bed just to be with Him for a few minutes, even when we had a house full of company. I now sensed His presence when I drew near to Him, something certainly new to me. It was all a wonder to me, a miracle. I was enthralled with the newness of knowing God and knowing that He knew me.

I had dealt with fears and depression for years, not the kind that immobilizes, but the nagging cloud that dulls the vitality of life, the kind that blocks out the sunshine in one's life. Now it was gone. For an entire week I was free of any depression or anxiety. A week later, however, it was back. A familiar sensation of feeling shaky and somewhat disoriented slithered over me. Not having expected it ever to be there again, I felt that I had been abandoned by God. I rushed to my bedside and dropped to my knees and cried out to Him. "Where are You? Your Word says that You would never leave me or forsake me." I was devastated and frightened that I had lost what had become so precious to me in such a short period of time. Was it over? Was it all a lie?

Just as I was considering that possibility, kneeling there

by my bed, I felt as if a blanket had been thrown over me, a blanket of warmth and love and comfort. The sense of Yeshua's presence was so strong that I opened my eyes fully expecting to see Him to be standing on my bed. He wasn't, of course, but the almost tangible sense of His caring for me was wrapped around me, restoring me to peace in Him. Thanksgiving flowed out of my heart with the relief that I was still His and He was still with me. I rose from my bedside with a deeper assurance that I really did belong to God. It would take several years before I received a diagnosis of hypoglycemia which was the cause of all those symptoms, and a few more until the Lord healed me of it but in the intervening time I learned to lean on His strength to get me through each episode. The Lord is a very present help in trouble.

While I have not heard the Lord's voice audibly since, I have continued to listen and hear God speak to me almost daily in a "still small voice," which is how the prophet Elijah described it. I later realized that the word "listen" or "hear" in Hebrew is the word "sh'ma which is the first word of the most often prayed prayer in Judaism: "Here O Israel, the Lord our God is one God." I also learned that the word for one (echad) is not a single unit but a compound or plural "one" as in several men making up one army, or many grapes making up one bunch. This explained to me the perplexing issue of why God is Genesis is recorded by Moses as saying, "Let US make man in OUR image." When God had spoken to me and had said, "Listen," had He said it in Hebrew I would have heard, "Sh'ma." What could be more Jewish than that?

Chapter 6

*T*elling my family was the first task at hand. I wanted to tell all my family and friends but I was concerned with how they would react? They would probably have the same objections I had initially, only it was less likely that they would hear the voice of God to help them over their doubts. Nevertheless, I knew I couldn't keep this to myself. Such a life changing experience must be shared with those you love and who love you, and besides it was bound to overflow quite naturally into any conversation I would have. There is very little that remains a private experience in a Jewish family anyway. It's part of the cultural norm to share one's life and decisions with family members.

My husband and I had discussed the book that Nancy had given me as we had some of the course material from the religion classes I was taking. "You're becoming an intellectual Christian," he had said to me after one of our discussion. It was more of a question than an observation. To him, as long as it was intellectual, it was acceptable. More than that would be questionable. I wasn't sure how he was going to take Jesus now being a part of my life – our lives. He was silent for a few moments when I told him and then said quietly, "I envy you your faith" and said no more at the time. Many more discussions would ensue over time.

Telling my parents, then in their 60's, was not going to be that easy, I expected. What Jewish parents welcome that kind of news? I decided the direct approach was best. "I have something I want to tell you. I've come to believe that Jesus is the Jewish Messiah," I explained some of what had happened briefly and then waited for their reaction. After the initial shock of my declaration, Dad responded first. He stood up, came over to me and pulling me out of the chair, gave me a very big hug, telling me that if this is what gives me happiness, then he supported it. I couldn't have been more surprised – or relieved. Much later I would find out why he was so open to the idea of my believing in Jesus. Mom on the other hand, always supportive and loving, found this very foreign to her orthodox Jewish upbringing but since my brother was following some guru somewhere in India, Jesus was at least Jewish and somehow seemed well, American.

Chapter 7

*T*he only Bible I had was one that had arrived unbeck-
oned when I had forgotten to send the card back from
the Book of the Month Club years before. Maxine informed
me that that translation wasn't kosher as far as she was concerned though that wasn't the term she used, and I needed to
have a New American Standard Study Bible. She told me
where there was a Christian bookstore and being a booka-
holic anyway, I went in search of a proper Bible. While it
had been several weeks that I'd officially been a Believer,
and I continued to be thrilled with my new relationship with
God, considering entering the Gentile world of 'church' was
entirely alien to me. It was culturally "other" to the point of
anxiety. What would Grandmom Jenny say if she knew, I
thought, ashamed that I was glad that she wasn't here anymore to find out.

I'd had a number of gentile friends, but that wasn't about
God, that was about tennis or a book discussion group, or a
cooking class. This was different. We were dealing with the
very foundation of my Jewishness now that we were talking
books about God, especially a Bible.

I entering the book store tentatively, fighting the feeling that I was being a traitor to my people. Even the jingle
of the bell on the door sounded *goyisha* (gentile) to me.

Books had always been my friends, since I had been an avid reader from the age of seven. But as my eyes scanned the titles they might as well have said 'Nazi Germany" to me, or "Crusades." I wanted to turn and run. What was a nice Jewish girl like me doing looking at books with titles about "The Cross" or "Sanctification," whatever that was. *Weren't those about killing Jews?*

Just as I was about to bolt for the door a tiny woman with an English accent suddenly perched herself in front of me like a bird landing on a branch and said pleasantly, "Hello Dearie." Not knowing what else to say to her, I said, "Hello. How are you?" "Praising the Lord, Dearie," she responded enthusiastically, "Praising the Lord." What's the appropriate response to that, I wondered when she asked, "Can I help you find something?" "A Bible," I said. "I need a Bible. And if you have any books for new Jewish believers, that would be good," I answered, trying not to let my nervousness show. "Oh you're a new Jewish believer, are you?" she said peering up into my face as if checking to see that what I said was true. "Y'look Jewish, y'do," she confirmed. I wasn't sure if she thought that was a good thing or a bad thing to her. My palms were beginning to sweat.

"Here are the Bibles," she said leading me down an aisle. "Do you know which kind you want?" I told her a New American Standard. I chose one and then asked again about the books for Jewish believers. Surely I wasn't the only Jew who believed. Someone must have written something, I tried to reassure myself. "Oh, no Dearie," she chirped, Y'don't need anything different. It's all the same, Jewish or not." Well, that may have been easy for her to say, but as for me I was still feeling increasingly like I as in foreign territory. Then suddenly she bent down and pulled a book off of a bottom shelf and said. "Oh here, this may do it for you," as she handed me a copy of a book with the unlikely title of *Corned Beef, Knishes & Christ* by someone with a very Jewish name. Moishe Rosen maybe.

I immediately felt better. Kin had been there before me. Surely there was hope in that book that I wasn't alone. After all, except for Marlene, the only other Jew to my knowledge who ever thought that Yeshua was actually the Messiah was Yeshua himself.

One day I decided I needed to go to church to see what went on there. Maxine had repeatedly invited me to hers so I decided to give it a try. Still uncomfortable with the whole idea of "going to church" I told my husband that I was going to the fabric store one Sunday morning as that always took me a long time. I doubted that God would approve of my lying – would He overlook it since it was about going to church. Once I went it was easy to return again.

Within a few months of my attending the church, they announced that they were having a baptism service. While my new Gentile friends seem to think this was a "Christian" thing done only by believers in Jesus, I knew this to be as Jewish as keeping kosher. This was a *mikveh*, a bath for the purpose of being ritually clean in order to come before God. My grandmother's Synagogue had a *mikveh* where those who belonged to the Synagogue would periodically go in order to maintain the cleanliness rules of *Torah*. The women would go monthly or anyone else after they may have touched a dead person or anything considered "unclean." Jews would also go into the *mikveh* upon entering a new season in their lives, such as before a marriage, to symbolically wash away the old. Also a *mikveh* would take place for someone who wanted to become a Jew and had gone through the conversion process. It was obvious to me that the first Believers in Yeshua who were, of course, Jews would enter into a ritual bath on the occasion of entering a deeper relationship with God. It was a symbol of cleansing themselves of an old life in order to follow the Messiah and keep God's commandments anew. That was just what I wanted to do.

The night of my baptism was a stormy night. Mom had difficulty coming into a church altogether and this didn't help. To Mom, the lightning zig-zagging across the huge stained glass window in the front of the church, just above the baptismal pool, was clearly evidence that my grandmother, whom she presumed to be in heaven, was letting us know she did not approve. Eventually the storm subsided just in time for me to be immersed in the water. It was a touching and meaningful moment for me and I felt a great connection between myself and my God. I felt His *shalom,* His peace and His presence. All was well in my world. All was well, that is, until the next morning.

Chapter 8

I was awakened at 7:00 a.m. by the ringing phone insistently demanding that I answer it. I sleepily reached for it and managed to croak 'Hello." It was Sam. From the sound of his voice I knew that all was not well, at least not with him. "Since 6:15 this morning my phone has not stopped ringing," he ṣaid in a voice that I'd never heard him use before. "I'm going to ask you one question. I just want a yes or a no. Were you or were you not baptized in a church last night?" As surprised as I was with his confrontation and the obvious tension in his voice, I simply answered, "Yes I was."

Uncharacteristic for Sam who was usually a man of reason and even tempered demeanor he began to say with great articulation, "I will not take responsibility for this. I will not take responsibility for this." I suppose my own reaction might have been interpreted as disrespect. It wasn't meant to be as I had high regard for my Rabbi and friend Sam, but my response was the only one that made sense to me. "You can't. Only God can." He said that we'd talk about this later and hung up.

During all the time that I was becoming a Believer, Sam and Havah had been away on a six-month sabbatical in Israel. For understandable reasons I had declined to renew my position as secretary to the Religious School Committee though I didn't share those reasons with the Committee. My husband, while he never said one thing that could have been interpreted as a prohibition against my new-found faith, had asked me not to tell the children, nor our Rabbi nor our Synagogue friends. I negotiated being able to answer only the questions that I was asked.

Shortly after Sam and Havah returned from Israel, they had come over one evening for dinner. I had mentioned nothing, of course. Sam, who shared our enthusiasm for books, and enjoyed perusing the bookshelves which lined one wall of our living room, found a relatively new book to our collection entitled, *Christianity is Jewish*, by Edith Schaeffer, the wife of the man who wrote *The God Who is There*. With all the books on our shelves, Sam had just happened to notice that one. He pulled it out for a moment and I watched him flip through the pages, check out the Table of Contents, and then put it back. Since he had not asked any questions, I said nothing and neither did he. Now, however, word had gotten out within the community that I had been baptized. Now he knew why the book was there.

Within a few days my friend and weekly tennis partner called to say that she could no longer keep our tennis date. Other phone calls that would have come about various Synagogue matters ceased as if a ban had been placed on calling me. It may or may not have been an official ban and I probably would have reacted the same way had it been some one else and not me, but I knew what I had done was considered as having defected. I would be thought of as having betrayed my Judaism and my fellow Jews. My heart hurt. I knew just how they were feeling and I fully understood why they reacted this way. Centuries of misunderstanding and misrepresentation of Who He is was now separating me from my friends. I longed for them to understand that I had met the God of Abraham, Isaac and Jacob through Messiah Yeshua, but I knew that that was not a probability. There would not be an opportunity for an audience with Sam or my friends in which I could tell them how much Yeshua meant to me and have them accept that. Had I not have had the experiences that God had led me through I would not have been open to hearing it either. I had to leave them to God.

Two weeks later I received a call from my friend Carolyn asking if she could come to see me. Of course. I looked forward to her visit since I hadn't seen any of my Synagogue friends during this time. She came bearing a small book in hand, warmly hugged me hello and handing me the book, said enthusiastically, "The confirmation class started asking questions about, well, you know. They wanted to know how we can be sure that Jesus wasn't the Messiah. So Sam sent for these books from Hebrew Union College in New York." I knew that Sam calling Hebrew Union was like summoning help from on high on a great matter of urgency. With 20 or so teenagers asking this question, it was obvious that something had to be done. I looked at the title that said something like "How We Know that Jesus Is Not the Messiah." She encouraged me to read it and seemed quite certain that once I had, I would return to a sound mind, renounce this false Messiah, and things could get back to normal. She gave me another quick hug and left.

It didn't take me long to read the booklet. It was about 50 pages in length with Scriptures predicting the coming of the Messiah (and leaving out, I noticed, several that, in my estimation, would have succinctly pointed to Yeshua) and what He was to accomplish, such as bringing peace. I knew He had brought peace to me and millions personally, but I knew that the universal peace expected of the Messiah would not be accomplished until He returned and fulfilled *all* Scripture. The booklet also contained commentaries from Rabbis throughout the centuries and had a brief history of some of the horrendous treatment of Jews by men who had claimed to be Christians. I, too, needed to summon help from on high to determine how I was to respond. Reading the little book certainly didn't shake my faith that Yeshua was indeed the Jewish Messiah; it said what I had expected it to say, what I too would have said if I had been in their place.

I longed for them to know Him as I did, to know that this gentle and kind God of ours could never have brought about those atrocities which were done in His Name by evil people – people who had hate in their hearts and not His love. I knew that they didn't understand and I wanted with all my heart to bridge the gap between myself and them, and even more between Him and them. I took my Bible and went and sat on the grass under my favorite tree to talk it over with the Lord.

"Lord, you know what that booklet says. I'm not doubting that You are who You said you are. But what would you say to me in response to what I just read, Scripture verses and all? And what can I tell them?" I opened my Bible, not sure where I was going to look, but I knew the answers had to come from there somewhere. I opened the book and my eyes fell on the page before me, and there in the words of the prophet Ezekiel I read:

"Thus says the Lord God, 'It is not for your sake, O house of Israel, that I am about to act, but for My holy name, which you have profaned among the nations where you went. And I will vindicate the holiness of My great name which has been profaned among the nations, which you have profaned in their midst. Then the nations will know that I am the Lord, declares the Lord God, when I prove Myself holy

among you in their sight.... Then I will sprinkle clean water on you, and you will be clean. I will cleanse you from all your filthiness (sins) and from all your idols. Moreover, I will give you a new heart and put a new spirit within you and I will remove the heart of stone from your flesh and give you a heart of flesh. And I will put My Spirit within you and cause you to walk in My statutes, and you will be careful to observe My ordinances." (Ezek. 36:25-27)

As sure as I was leaning against the massive trunk of the tree, I knew I could lean on the Bible to give me the truth. It was a hard word and a reassuring word at the same time but I knew that it was true and I knew that God had led me to that passage. I recalled when I had used His name in a way that did not honor Him, that the Commandments say we must not take His name in vain. I recalled that it was not so long ago that I had lived entirely independent of God, never giving Him a thought. I knew that there had been things in my life of which I would have been greatly ashamed had they been known to anyone other than myself. I had never considered, nor had I heard in all my years as a Jewess, that my life was to be a reflection of God's goodness and holiness. Abraham and his family were to make God known to the people around them, wherever He would send them. There was nothing until recently that would have caused anyone to consider how God fit into their lives because of what they saw in mine.

I also knew, however, that my life was a fulfillment of those verses, that God had made me clean. He had put a new spirit and a new heart within me. I was a changed person. Whereas before I had no regard for, or interest in, His commandments or the Bible, now they were my daily pleasure and my source of wisdom. He had caused me to observe His ordinances.

And I knew that as real as these words were to me, without the Spirit of God to make it real it would be little more than antiquated literature to others, just as it had once been to me. God had indeed put His Spirit within me and had caused my disappointed and dull heart to become alive and to desire to please Him. At that moment, God placed within my heart a desire to bring honor to His name. His Word was now a pleasure to me, both to know it and to do it. And it was all His doing. Would I be able to tell all this to my Rabbi, my friends, and the Confirmation class who were at least asking some good questions?

I didn't answer the booklet. Perhaps I should have, but my faith in Yeshua was too new to me and too precious for it to have become a matter of argument, or even intellectual debate. It was too treasured, like something so valuable as to be cherished protectively, to have it exposed, even to those I loved, who were not likely to have regard for it – or Him – as I did. Perhaps one reason for my writing this book is to take responsibility for my reluctance to enter into the confrontation I anticipated. I never was one for conflict. Trying to explain to one's Rabbi that you have met the resurrected Messiah is no small challenge. I would like to have given my friends an explanation of what had happened to me. There was some attempt to try and get me to change my mind. But no one ever asked me why, or how come, or what happened to me that I came to believe in Yeshua. Perhaps they will read this book and know.

What Marlene had said to me about how the Holy Spirit inside of me would teach me the things of God, was now becoming my daily experience. While my desire was, and remains still, for my Jewish people to return to God so that He is not extraneous to their lives, my heart overflowed with joyful gratitude to God for making me His, and for bringing me into a relationship with Him. The Lord had caused the words of the Hebrew Prophet Ezekiel to become my very own experience. In the insignificance of my own life in the vast scheme of things, God Himself had taken note of me and had revealed His Son to me. There is no greater joy on earth than to know Him and to know the reassuring love of God. He offers the same opportunity to anyone who wishes to come to Him!

Section Two

My Brother,
Michael Lane

Chapter 9

One would never have anticipated that my brother Michael would have been a candidate for a counter culture. He was not some aggressive or adverse personality. He was, and still is, a rather gentle and congenial person, warm and likeable, and easy to get along with. He was, however, as most of us are, a product of his social milieu. Though only a few years my junior, in his teenage years he went in an entirely different direction than I had. I was a product of the 50's, he of the 60's. The major reason for the change was The Pill. Michael and his peers more than any other people before them saw themselves as having unlimited control over their lives because of drugs and birth control. Birth control pills changed their morality. At the same time, other substances, such as LSD, could bring them to some supposed higher consciousness and an awareness of things never considered by their parents, or for that matter their older siblings. The "anything-goes" attitude and the apathy that came with the drugs and the birth control pills pulled Michael and his childhood friends in with the force of an undertow. To them, however, the ride was glorious and freeing. At the age of 18 Michael left the real estate business he'd been involved in with our father, while building the ground level of what was to be come Society Hill in

Philadelphia, in order to become a "Hippie."

He didn't start out to be a Hippie, he just took a trip across country to California with Jimmy and Billy and a few others, the same buddies that he had played with since he was little. You can take a trip and return and say, "Well, that was nice," but in this case Michael's entire life was altered. Once in California, the freedom from the restraints that generally characterize society formed an alternative society and the Hippie culture was born. Living in Haight Ashbury in San Francisco, Michael became a part of a social revolution led by Timothy Leary. They'd found utopia. This was the way to live. They "tuned out and turned on" and lived in drug-and sex-filled days with a deep sense of loyalty to the group and the excitement that comes from any revolutionary movement.

Michael and his friends were among the first of a generation who put things in their bodies and manipulated their hormones and brain waves in order to reach a higher state of consciousness. It became a way of life for them. Soon, kids from all over the country began to leave home in droves and descend upon "The Haight." Michael and his friends considered that these new kids were pseudo-hippies, wanna-be's – not the real thing. They held a funeral for the Real Hippie, casket and all (an incident which made the Encyclopedia regarding the 1960's, we've been told). Then Michael, Jimmy and a select group of friends took off for Hawaii where they planned to live out the rest of their lives in relative isolation, eating whatever nature provided for them.

In spite of all this, somehow Michael managed to remain a relatively dutiful son. As detached from normal life as he was, he would occasionally hitch a ride into town, drop the few coins he kept for such occasion into a pay phone and place a collect call my parents, in order to let them know that he was all right. His living this way and so far away was very difficult on my parents who never knew when or for that matter *if* they would see him again as he had no intention of returning – ever.

Then Michael got sick. Very sick. When he didn't get any better after the expected amount of time, and in fact seemed worse, Jimmy had enough sense to call my parents who wired money to fly them both home. Jimmy came too to take care of Michael on the flight home, though Michael would later report that Jimmie was too high on drugs to be of much help to him. When Michael stepped off the plane onto the tarmac he was shirtless, brown and barefoot, and carried the pillow that he had left with years before. The color of his skin, we soon realized, was not just from his tan but from the jaundice that was also evident in his eyes. Mom felt his head and found that it was burning hot. We got him into the car and drove directly to my cousin Dick, who is a doctor. Dick had Michael admitted immediately to the hospital, with hepatitis and dehydration. "Another day or two," Dick soberly informed Mom, "and he might not have made it."

With Dick's care and six weeks of imposed bed rest Michael did make it. Once he was well enough to be getting bored, I brought him a guitar and began to teach him how to play a few chords and some good folks picks and strums. It was, after all, the 60's and one was almost obligated to learn to play a guitar. I had known just about enough to supplement our income while my husband was in law school, by teaching the guitar to kids who knew less than I did. With nothing else to do Michael began to get the hang of it and soon was much better than I. When he grew well, within the next year, he gave up the idea of returning to Hawaii and went off to Boston to study guitar at Berkely School of Music.

<<>>

73

Even though Michael had returned to society, more or less, and was attending music school in Boston, he still maintained the ever elusive quest for higher consciousness and the meaning of life. It always seemed to be just one more experience away – maybe the next one would be the real one. One day while walking down "Com Ave" in Boston with some friends, he heard someone speaking on a street corner: "If you want peace," said an Indian man in a saffron colored robe and a turban, "Come to me." This guru was offering hope and "light," knowing that, with the Beatles as an example, followers would come.

The guru touched Michael on his forehead and suddenly with his eyes closed Michael saw a flash like a great white light and became a believer on the spot. This guru was actually a spokesman for a fifteen-year old wonder called Guru Maharaji. Maharaji's message was basic Hinduism. Michael began meditating and became a vegetarian. He still took drugs (though never hard, mainlining drugs) and smoked a lot of marijuana. Between the LSD and other drugs and now the occultic meditation, he parked his brain somewhere and rarely used it much any more. When I did hear from him, most of his conversation was reduced to simple sentences like, "Hey, what's happening?" Or when I tried to impart some wisdom to him, it was, "Lonnie, what do you know?" indicating that I knew nothing because I wasn't "enlightened."

The Divine Light Mission, which was Maharaji's organization was largely comprised of Jewish kids seeking truth and the reality of God. Unfortunately, many of them got stuck right there. A number of Michael's friends are still *premies*, followers of Maharji today. This was no small movement, relatively speaking, at that time. At one point they hired three jumbo jets, which Michael was in charge of hiring, and flew several hundred followers of Maharaji to India to live at the foot hills of the Himalayas where presumably they would become more Enlightened. Michael spent 6 weeks in India in his search, but the most he seemed to come home with, that I could observe, was dysentery.

Later on, it was determined that Maharaji was to usher in the Millenium, having something to do with the introduction of the Age of Aquarius. This was a wholly distorted interpretation of Biblical prophesy which has nothing at all to do with the Age of Aquarius, but no one was knowledgeable enough to know that. By this time, Michael was living in Denver, the Mission's headquarters, and was now in charge of renting the Astrodome in Houston where the Millenium celebration would take place and of securing housing for the participants. He reserved every hotel in Houston for the designated week of the celebration since they expected many thousands to attend.

A group of Christians stationed themselves outside the Astrodome who had apparently been praying for quite a while about the event. In the end, far fewer people came than had been expected and several things that had taken place had caused Michael to be disenchanted. He began to doubt that Maharaji held all the answers.

Shortly afterward, Michael moved back to Pennsylvania and just happened to move in with a group of hippies who lived less than a mile from my house. After years of his being away from home and living all over the country and elsewhere in the world, for him to move this close to me, considering that I had been praying for him, God had to have had something to do with it. Michael had put so much of his life into Maharaji and the life style that he had been living, that he still held onto the meditation and the whole Hindu mindset, though his confidence in Maharaji was shaken.

One day Michael had a discussion with my son Rick, then around age 14, who said to Michael, "You say that

Maharaji says that he's not God, but Yeshua says that He is, so why do you keep following someone who is less than God?" Later Michael would tell me that he gave that much thought, but my belief in Yeshua continued to be as alien to him as a pork sandwich and a glass of milk would be to an Orthodox Jew and we had many "My spiritual experience is better than yours" discussions. I saw Michael's religion as having more to do with his body and soul than knowing God in his Spirit, The activities he performed, such as the meditation, the yoga positions, the chanting, and the use of incense weren't really bringing him to a true knowledge of or relationship with God such as I had come to know. I continued to pray for him, knowing God would have to make it real to him; I certainly wasn't able to.

One day, when a few feet of snow had blanketed the east coast and no one was going anywhere, I looked out the window to see Michael's little VW bug chugging up my quarter of a mile unplowed driveway. How he had driven there when it was almost impossible in the snow? It had to be an act of God, I decided, so I figured something was up. At that moment, the Lord spoke to me and told me to be quiet and not to argue with Michael about our spiritual experiences. I know that when God says "listen" to me, He's about to do something, so I just listened. I let Michael do most of the talking. Eventually, he ran out of things to talk about now that I wasn't fueling it with my own remarks and found that there wasn't that much to say after all.

At some point we went into the kitchen to have some apple sauce cake I had just made, along with a cup of herb tea. I said a little prayer, thanking God for being there with us, since He was always there with me, for Michael arriving safely in the snow, and for the food. When I looked up from my prayer I was surprised to see tears streaming down Michael's cheeks. "What's the matter?" I asked. Almost in a whisper, after a moment he answered, "I didn't see anyone,

I didn't hear anyone, I just knew Jesus was there. When you said 'Thank you for being with us,' I felt His Presence. He touched me and...." He hesitated a moment, wiping away the tears, and then said, "I... I know Who He is!"

It was that simple. It all happened in a few seconds. God in His graciousness had revealed Himself to Michael. With all his spiritual experiences, one encounter with Yeshua, and Michael had found what he had been looking for all these years – the Living God. That day was Michael's birthday. We had both come to know the Lord on our birthdays. What better gift could anyone ever receive, than for God to give you Himself on your birthday.

Getting Michael out of the life he was living, however, presented some interesting challenges. From the first day he entered into a relationship with Yeshua his life radically changed. But he had been meditating for so long that it was as addictive as the pot he was smoking. I challenged him to not meditate for ten days and to start reading the Book of John. I gave him a Bible and he agreed to do it, though it was very difficult for him not to be meditating. Generally speaking, on an emotional level, meditation keeps one in a passive mindset, and any stress at all is hard to deal with and sends the person scampering back to a meditative state rather than deal with the stressor and resolve it. In that sense, it's addictive since one is dependent on the meditation. What we didn't realize then was that he was under the control of some powerful demonic forces which were not interested in having him involved with Yeshua, and he was under a great deal of spiritual oppression.

I called the 700 Club, a TV ministry show which also had a prayer line, to ask them to pray for Michael as he was having a difficult time. A woman by the name of Esther

Lane, with the same last name as ours answered the phone that day. I explained Michael's situation, then she said with excitement, "Well, I asked the Lord for a Jewish soul just this morning, so he'll be ok. Let's pray." And she prayed indeed, pulling down the power of God on his behalf. I was greatly encouraged.

Several months later I was at the Academy of Music in Philadelphia. The Lord said to me, "The woman sitting directly in front of you is Esther Lane." I tapped her on the shoulder and asked her if she was Esther Lane. She was! She remembered my phone call and was delighted to know that Michael was doing well in the Lord and had been set free, but not as delighted as I was that God had blessed me with yet another of His thoughtful experiences like meeting her.

Michael began to spend time with my believing friends and me. One day Marge told Michael, "I was praying for you this morning and the Lord told me to tell you that you have authority over the devil and his demons in the name of Yeshua. You can tell them to leave in His name and they must obey." Two nights later Michael again sensed a demonic presence. Suddenly his dog, Miss Muffet, began jumping as she lay on the floor as if she was being tormented. Michael took authority over what was happening and told the demon who was bothering Muffet to get out of her and get out of the house and leave him, in Jesus name. He actually saw, in the spirit, a gray and ugly demon come out of Muffet and go down the stairway and out of the house. It never bothered him or Muffet again. From that day on, any time he tried to put a marijuana cigarette in his mouth he'd get nauseous. The Lord had taken care of the demons and the drugs and had completely set him free of addictions. Within a short period of time, Michael moved out of the hippie house and abandoned that entire life style, and began Bible college.

<<>>

Michael had never done well in school as a kid. He had been diagnosed with *Petit Mal*, a mild form of epilepsy which caused him to lose awareness of his surroundings for short periods of time, making it very difficult to follow what was being taught in school. Between that and the use of LSD and marijuana which, according to medical documentation, do destroy brain cells, Michael had difficulty expressing himself or following a thought through to its conclusion. But soon, however, God healed his brain entirely. It is nothing short of a miracle that Michael got straight A's in Bible school for the two years he attended.

A further miracle is that Michael can tell you the location of almost any verse in the Bible. He has an incredible ability to teach extemporaneously on any passage of Scripture and explain how it relates to Yeshua or Israel or the Jewish people, in both the New and the Old Covenants. He has been sought after for his teachings on the Jewish roots of Christianity and specifically on the Feasts of the Lord – the celebrations of *Passover, Rosh Hashana, Yom Kippor, Succout* and *Shavout*. After hearing him teach on the Feasts he was asked by a Chinese Bible College in New York to do a two day seminar, which was video taped and then dubbed into Chinese. The tapes were then taken to the underground Church in China where vast numbers serve the Lord secretly under threat of severe persecution should they be found to be Christians.

What the Lord has done in Michael's life is what could be called "a sign and a wonder." The God of Abraham, Isaac and Jacob took a hippie who was lost to society and to his Jewishness, who was barely able to express himself beyond simple thoughts, and has worked in his life to use him to affect the lives of many, even in different parts of the world, to teach them of the Hebrew roots of their Christianity. Michael's mental ability is tantamount to the many healings recorded in the New Testament when "Yeshua went about doing good and healing all who were oppressed by the devil." Like the man who'd been healed and said, "I was blind but now I see" and another who said, "I was lame, but now I can walk," Michael knows what it is to be rescued by the God of Abraham, Isaac and Jacob from a pathway leading to eventual destruction. He agrees that once he was lost, but now he's been found.

Section 3

My Father
George Ezra Lane

Chapter 10

When I first told my parents about my belief in Yeshua, Dad's reaction was not what I had anticipated. As a young boy, he had often been beaten up on the way home from school by some Catholic kids who called him a Christ killer, the very name that my son had been called. When Dad had gotten up and walked over to where I was sitting and pulled me out of the chair I wasn't at all sure what he was going to do until he put his arms around me, gave me a hug and said, "If this is what makes you happy, then I'm happy for you." His words were most unusual for a Jewish father who's daughter had just told him she believes in Jesus, especially with his background. Mom, on the other hand, looked like she was in shock but said nothing that could be interpreted as rejection either of what I was telling her or of me for believing it. That's my mom!

It was natural for me to share my enthusiasm for my new life in the Lord with my parents as we talked on the phone or visited. Mom only half listened, preoccupied with how foreign this would sound to her orthodox mother. Dad asked a few questions every once in a while and remained curiously supportive. I answered his questions as well as I could and then one day I suggested that he come to the Sunday school class I was attending, where he might find some of those answers. In time, to my delight, Dad started going to the class with me.

In the past, before I'd become a Believer, the tendency of Christians to want everyone else to become one was very distasteful and even fearful to me as a Jew. Now that I understood that God, the Creator of Life, had come as God's own Son so that He could take upon Himself, by His death, the punishment that was due, not only to Jews, but to all mankind, I knew that it was God's heart that stirred within me, wanting to draw others to Himself. I also knew that much hardship had come upon Jews, as well as many Gentiles, who were cruelly abused by many misguided and evil men who used the name of the Lord to do to others what the Lord Himself would never have sanctioned. It has often been a source of great sadness to me that the Lord has been so misrepresented to my people by those who say they are His but their deeds prove otherwise. My knowledge of Him is that He is only good and good only!! I so wanted Dad to accept this truth as his own so that he could enter into an actual relationship with God like the one I now had.

It was well known in our family that Dad would go almost anywhere for a good cup of coffee and a donut. I often wondered if the fact that I had happened to mention that coffee and donuts were served at the beginning of the class might have had something to do with his attending. For whatever reason, for more than a year he met me every Sunday morning at the Sunday School class. But never would he step foot into the sanctuary for the service that followed the class. That would be "going to church." That would be a *shondah* (worthy of shame). He was a Jew. He wasn't going "to church." Yet strangely, he continued to attend the Sunday School class.

Michael was planning to attend a conference of Messianic Judaism at Messiah College. Each year 1000 or so Jewish and Gentile Believers came together to worship the Lord and to learn of Him in His original Jewish context. Michael invited Dad to go with him and since he was always up for spending quality time with his children Dad agreed to go. I had taken my children to the seashore the same week. As I was leaving the beach on our last day at the end of the week, just as it was also Michael and Dad's last day at the conference, the Lord spoke to me and clearly said, "Your father has accepted me and has been baptized." My first response was to shout "Halleluia!" However, not sure that I wasn't telling myself what I wanted to hear, I knew I would have to wait to find out if it was true.

We had been home from the shore for about a half hour when the phone rang. It was Dad. The questions sprang into my mind immediately: Did he really accept the Lord and was he actually baptized? Before I could ask anything Dad announced as if I'd asked it, "Yes I did and yes I was!" "Yes, you did what?" I questioned, my excitement growing. "Yes, I did accept the Lord and yes, I was baptized," he said with obvious delight in his voice. I *had* heard from the Lord!

He began to tell me the story. He had sat through days of workshops and lectures about the fulfillment of the Scriptures by Yeshua's sinless life, atoning death and resurrection and about the things that God is doing today in Israel in fulfillment of Biblical prophesy. He had enjoyed the evenings of inspiring Messianic Jewish music which touched his heart deeply. During the meals he had enjoyed lively discussions with Jews from all over America, from Israel and other nations around the world. They had reminded him of the discussions he had heard as a child in his grandfather's house. His *Zaida* (grandfather), being a Rabbi, had had many discussions with the men in his *shull* (Synagogue) around his dining room table over a *glezala tay* (glass of tea, no doubt with a lump of sugar tucked over their teeth). These were among some of my father's happiest memories.

As he had listened to the conference discussions he had come to understand more and more until, like a light being turned on so that he could see, like someone sweeping away the rubble of confusion to reveal a mosaic beneath, he suddenly knew without a doubt that Yeshua was, in fact, the Messiah! The realization of the truth of it settled into his heart like something he had always known. It just felt, he said, like he had "come home."

He had come to this realization the morning that the conference was to end. During last lunch of the conference people were saying goodbye until next year when, Lord willing, they would see each other again. But Dad was on another mission. He knew that he had to be baptized. Having grown up in his grandfather's orthodox *shull* he well knew what a *mikveh* was and felt strongly that, as a good Jewish man, he needed to observe what Yeshua had said was a good Jewish thing to do. But who was to baptize him?

At the Messianic conference each year a service is held in which everyone who wishes to enter the waters of *mikveh* is baptized in the river which runs through the College where the conference was held. With hundreds of conference attendees sitting on the banks watching, one by one people wade into the water, tell their story of their commitment to Yeshua, and are immersed by two of the elders. Dad, however, had missed the opportunity earlier that week.

He had looked around the cafeteria where everyone was having their farewell lunch until his eyes fell upon the one man at the conference who bore a striking resemblance to his *Zaida* with a bushy and long white beard reaching half way down his chest. Dad approached him, knowing he was the Rabbi of a Messianic congregation, and asked if he would baptize him. "But I'm leaving for the airport in 45 minutes. I don't have time. I'm going to change my clothes now and leave," Rabbi Eleazar replied. Being a man who was always quick with a solution, Dad said, "If we go to the river right now, it will only take 10 minutes. I won't even change my clothes." Apparently Dad's earnestness was enough for Rabbi Eleazar to agree to do it, and off to the river they went, followed by a fairly large group of folks who had evidently heard what was about to take place. Everyone loves a baptism.

They arrived at the river, Dad in his new suit and Rabbi Eleazar in khakis and a shirt. They were taking off their shoes when Dad, the most modest man in the world (I never even saw him in his underwear in the 21 years I lived with him), asked if anyone minded if he took off his new suit so that it wasn't ruined. No one minded, so he stripped down to his shorts, waded out into the river with Rabbi Eleazar who then immersed him in the water in the name of the Father, the Son and the Holy Spirit. "I felt so joyful I leaped out of the water with a shout 'cause I knew I finally fully belonged to the Lord," Dad concluded. From that day on he lived with and for Yeshua.

One day, in the course of our conversation I asked Dad, "How come you responded so positively when I first told you that I believed in Yeshua?" That began yet another of Dad's stories, one that he was reluctant to share at first, having held it in the secret place of his heart for so many years.

It was during the Korean war and things were very hard financially. There were a great many problems in his life at that time and he was feeling hopeless and didn't know where to turn. On the way to work each day he listened to the radio in the car. He had found a program on which the speaker encouraged people and gave them hope to carry on so Dad tuned in each day. The man also spoke about Jesus. Dad listened for the hope part, trying to ignore the Jesus part.

One day, overcome with despair, he pulled over to the side of the road and cried out in sudden desperation, "Jesus, you're the only one left. If you're really there, can you help me?" Immediately he felt a warmth, more like heat cover his whole body, and then he began to cry. He cried and cried until he could cry no more. Then he grew quiet and peace came. The release had come as a result of crying out to Jesus, he knew that. From then on, he had what he could only describe as a continual awareness of Jesus being near him, something he'd certainly never had before that day. He had never shared the experience with anyone until the day he told me about it many years later. He had kept it to himself knowing that no one in his family or among his friends, all Jewish, would have accepted the fact that he had talked to Jesus, let alone that he thought Jesus had heard him and responded to him. When I had come to tell him about my own experience with Yeshua, it had caused a quietly burning ember to suddenly flash into a flame of new hope in his heart that he would finally be able to outwardly embrace the Jesus who had strengthened him in his desperate weakness many years before.

When our family began attending a Messianic Synagogue, it was meeting in a hotel. However, as the congregation grew, it became clear that we needed our own "home." At first it was difficult to locate a property, but Dad, being a real estate broker, found a suitable building, negotiated the transaction and, in fact, put up his own money to purchase it for the congregation, for which they reimbursed him within six months. Once the purchase was complete, there was a lot of remodeling that needed to be done in order to turn the seafood restaurant into a Synagogue with a sanctuary, classrooms, offices and a kitchen. Dad pitched in as foreman of the job. Another member, Bob, and his sons also worked with him as did a number of other skilled men from the congregation. "I'm helping to build a Temple for the Lord," Dad often said with much personal satisfaction – he loved doing it. He was working not so much for the congregation, but "for the Lord," as he said. The motive of his heart was certainly in the right place. I have no doubt but that the Lord was pleased.

Shortly after the construction of the Synagogue building was completed we had our first service there, much to the joy of everyone. I think Dad had the greatest sense of accomplishment in having done all this "for the Lord." Many from other Messianic congregations around the country came to celebrate with us. One woman, a nurse, was visiting with our parents while here for the celebration and noticed Dad's swollen ankles. She suggested he see Philip, one of the doctors in the congregation. Within a week, Philip had Dad admitted to the hospital for tests which revealed that he had done all that work with only one third of the normal blood supply to his heart, and that he needed open heart surgery for a double valve replacement immediately! The cardiologist explained to Dad, my mother, my brother and me the dangers of this operation. He could die on the table. On the other hand, if he didn't have the surgery, he couldn't assure that Dad would live another six months. We would have to make the choice. He suggested that Dad go home for a week to think about it. We thanked the doctor and asked if he would please leave us alone to discuss it.

As soon as the doctor left, Dad said, "OK, let's pray. Let's ask Yeshua what we should do." We began to pray and we all felt the presence of the Lord enter the room bringing His peace with Him, and we knew that it would be all right. Dad spoke first saying, "I feel Yeshua is with me and that He's telling me I should have the surgery and I'll be fine." We all agreed and thanked the Lord for looking after Dad and for protecting him. Dad had complete assurance as he cheerfully told the cardiologist, Dr. Dougherty, the next day that he would like to have the surgery that week if possible so that he could get on with his life. Dr. Dougherty was sure that Dad was in denial about the gravity of the situation. "Now, Mr. Lane, you have to realize what a critical decision this is and not make it too quickly." Dad replied again cheerfully, "It'll be OK, Doc. I'll be just fine. Let's just schedule it and do it." Dr. Doughtery went to Philip to tell him that he didn't think that Mr. Lane was dealing with reality. Phil assured him he was and that he was a man of great faith and if he felt God had told him he would be fine, then he would be. And so the surgery was scheduled for that week.

When one has heart valves replaced one has a choice of titanium valves or those made from pig gut which is very close to human heart tissue, but the thought of having non-kosher heart valves was where Dad drew the line. "I'll have the titanium. No pig is going to be inside of me. *Traif* (unkosher food) to fix my heart? Feh!" The surgery was a success. But from the day of the surgery, he sound like Peter Pan's alligator. He ticked. His titanium valves could always be heard when the room was quiet enough. His favorite Scripture verse came from the Hebrew prophet Jeremiah (31:31) in which God, in speaking to the Jewish people about the New Covenant, said that He would give them, "a new heart."

According to Dr. Dougherty, Dad's heart surgery would prolong his life for at least another ten years but instead he lived almost another seventeen. During which time, although he was retired, he taught English as a second language to foreigners and as a result received awards from International House. He painted a great number of still life oil paintings, becoming a consummate still life painter and with great affection for both show tunes and chamber music, Dad played his cello and the piano.

Dad also had a number of trips the emergency room

during the last few years as his heart valves began leaking, causing him to go into congestive heart failure. We would have to adjust ourselves to the possibility each time that we might loose him. But the next time we would come into the Critical Care unit to visit him, he would be sitting up in bed, telling the nurses about Yeshua or telling them a story about "the good old days." Always there was a story. (I've been told that I'm like my father in many ways. Telling this story is probably one of them.)

One day when he was 82 years young, Dad asked me to take him to an *Aish Torah* lecture on the topic of the "Bible Codes." These are equidistant letter sequence words, found primarily in the Torah, which reveal that it is possible that the names and specific facts about many people and events, if not every person, are hidden within the words of Torah in the original Hebrew. An Orthodox Jewish man with a Ph.D. in mathematics was to be giving the lecture. Dad could have gone by himself but he was beginning to be somewhat unstable on his feet and had fallen a few times and it was best to have someone with him. I was eager to share the experience with him as I knew that the lecture would be fascinating, which it proved to be. The probability of these hidden prophesies being valid reveal that the Mind of God is immeasurably far beyond anything that we humans are able to grasp. The lecturer made that point quite clearly. Dad and I wanted to add, "And yet He cares about each one of us so personally."

During intermission, on the way to the bathroom on his own, Dad fell in the hallway and was unable to get up. Since the lecture took place in the auditorium of the hospital where he had spent so much time, the nurses knew him. Someone came to get me in the lecture hall asking, "Is there a Lonnie Lane here?" When she told me what happened, I was very calm with what I knew was God's grace, His stabilizing, enabling peace. A young Rabbi who was in charge of the program that day was standing near me when the nurse came in to find me. He became very concerned. "I'll go with you," he offered.

The nurses got Dad into the emergency room. It was obvious that he was in great pain, having hurt the hip which had been replaced two years before after he had fallen down the steps. He had twisted himself to avoid hitting his beloved cello and had heard the snap of his hip as he did so. He had come through that surgery and the rehab with flying colors. Now it was that same hip which he had damaged in this fall. Nevertheless, since he knew that he was in God's hands he was at peace as he always was in one of his medical crises. He had often said, "I know Yeshua is with me. He's here always, walking with me the whole way, holding my hand." When they took him to X-ray to find out the damage, I walked back into the lecture room with Rabbi Micah to listen while I waited for Dad's return.

As we walked Rabbi Micah said, "He's obviously in much pain." He hesitated and then continued, "But his *neshuma* (soul or spirit) is so alive." It was the first of many times that he would say that; each time he seemed puzzled. As much religion as Rabbi Micah was involved in, meeting a man whose spirit was alive with the Spirit of God was recognizable to him, yet perplexing and apparently new to him, especially when it was undaunted by pain.

He asked me if there was anything he could do for Dad. "You can pray for him," I answered. "What's his mother's name?" he asked, to which I responded, "What does his mother have to do with this?" He looked very serious as he said, "When it's for healing, you have to know the mother's name." "Her name was Celia," I answered, "but just tell God you're praying for George. He'll know who he is."

Later, after Dad had been admitted and was in a hospital

room, Rabbi Micah stopped in to see how he was. Though he was still in considerable pain, Dad remained peaceful and always had a sense of humor, no matter what. Again Rabbi Micah, talking not about Dad's level of pain but about his peace, said to me, "But his *neshumah* is so alive."

Dad remained in the hospital. Rabbi Micah came to visit often, bringing him a *Chalah* (twisted bread) for the Sabbath. One day, on the tray table over Dad's bed lay a book which my brother Michael had just brought to him on the same subject as was the Bible Code lectures we'd attended. This book, however, added the fact that the name Yeshua is found many times in the Torah, appearing to validate His Messiahship. Since the cover of the book had Hebrew letters on it, it attracted Rabbi Micah's attention, so as nonchalantly as he could, he drifted around the room until he could read the title of the book which was facing Dad. When he saw the name of Yeshua in the title, I saw his expression change. He had just realized that we were Messianic Jews.

Never one to miss an opportunity for a good discussion about Yeshua, my brother began talking with Rabbi Micah. "I see you're reading the title of the book. What if Yeshua's name is revealed in the Torah as Messiah as this book says?" Rabbi Micah responded immediately. "If I found out that Yeshua was the Messiah I would have no trouble changing my membership and becoming a believer in him," he said, "but he's not." We offered to give him the book and I said that I would be interested in hearing his opinion of it. He agreed to take the book but declined to discuss it with us and he left with the book in hand. He continued to come periodically to visit my father, who never got out of the hospital.

Dad had again been making great progress with physical therapy as he had when his hip had been replaced two years before. We hoped that he would be out of the hospital soon. One day when I came to see him he was sleeping while my mother was reading in the chair beside him. It was the first time he didn't respond at all when I came in and called his name. Even if he was dozing he'd always wake up and smile at me and say, "Hiya, Lon." Mom said that he had been sleeping most of the afternoon and that she didn't want to disturb him. I leaned over to give him a kiss on the forehead and found that he was burning hot. I immediately called the nurse who took his temperature and within minutes he was whisked off to Intensive Care. We soon were told that he had pneumonia and a very high fever. That began a 26-hour vigil of the last day of my father's life.

I called my daughters, Ellen and Jenny, who came over immediately. Dad would periodically rouse enough to respond a little to us to let us know that he was aware that we were with him. He was unable to speak anymore though he was able to hear us. We called my son who lived in San Francisco and held the phone to Dad's ear so that Rick could talk to him, knowing that he was saying goodbye to his dearly loved Pop-Pop. When Dad heard his voice, his first-born grandson with whom he had a very special relationship from the time Rick was born, he seemed to come alive enough to say, "Rick?" Rick's name was the last word on Dad's lips.

We continued to talk to Dad, to reminisce with him, sing to him, pray for him again and again, and tell him how much we loved him. The nurses and doctors were very respectful of us during that long vigil, keeping the curtains closed around his bed and disturbing us as little as possible while they made him as comfortable as they could. Dr. Dougherty, came in and we had to comfort him as he was very moved by the thought of losing my father of whom he'd become very fond over the years since Dad's open heart surgery.

In the end, we weren't there when he finally breathed his

last breath. We had finally taken Mom home, twenty-six hours later, all of us exhausted. A nurse called shortly after we arrived at Mom's to tell her that Dad was gone. We knew he was altogether at peace now.

The next day as we were making the funeral arrangements, I received a call from Rabbi Micah. He had gone to visit my father and couldn't find him. "He passed away last night," I told him. Shocked, he immediately responded, "But his *neshuma* was so alive, how could that be?" I assured him that Dad's *neshumah* was indeed still alive, though I doubt that he believed me. I invited him to participate in the funeral, to say *Kaddish* (the mourners prayer which is really praise to God even in death). He said that he'd be honored, but he never came.

Those who did come, however, were family from all branches of both sides of the family: aunts, uncles, cousins and many, many friends, both mine and those of my parents. Several hundred people attended to honor the memory of my father. We had no Rabbi speak. We didn't need a Rabbi when we ourselves knew best what we wanted to say about Dad.

The day before the funeral, I was trying to envision what Dad would have wanted to have said at his own funeral. It came so clearly to me, as if Dad himself would say to me, "Lon, if you could only see Yeshua and if you could only see what life is like here ...tell them. Tell them about Yeshua." The sense was so strong that I decided to act on it and speak what I knew would shock some people, people I dearly love, who, as Jews, are not accustomed to having anyone talk with them about Yeshua, especially at a funeral. It was not my intent to shock them, only to share what was so dear to Dad – his Yeshua.

I spoke first as the oldest child, venturing to share with

these dear folks, some who had never heard it said aloud, that my father's life was one of difficulty and pain as a child and young man but one of security and strength in knowing that the God of Abraham, Isaac and Jacob was with him always after he came to know Yeshua as Messiah. Accompanied on the guitar, Michael sang a song that was Dad's favorite, one which Michael had written entitled "Covenant of Peace," taken from Isaiah 54. He introduced the song at the funeral telling them how we all had sung it to Dad several times in the hospital that last day. My cousin Mark, always articulate, spoke of what his Uncle George meant to him, and two of my children, Rick and Ellen also spoke of their love for their Pop-Pop, recalling memories in their lives with their grandfather.

At the *shiva* (time of mourning at the house of the bereaved) one woman came to me and said, "I heard what you said at the funeral. You have something that I don't have and I want it." We talked a little that day as I briefly shared my experience with knowing Yeshua with her. I didn't see her again until her own mother, who had been a friend of my parents for 60 years, died six months later. At her mother's *shiva* she accepted Yeshua as Lord of her own life and has walked with him since. It was good of God to reach out to her just as she was about to enter a prolonged and difficult time in her life. She, like Dad, knows that He is with her through those times. I trust that God has touched the hearts of others who heard us speak that day and that they, too, will come to know that He will always be with them, even into eternity. Dad would have wanted that.

Section 4

My Two Moms

My Mother –Nesbeth Lane
and
My mother-in-Law–
Sylvia Berg

Chapter 11

*T*wo Israeli businessmen were coming from New York to do business with my husband and were also coming to our home for dinner. I felt as if the Prime Minister himself was coming. There is something about being with Israeli's that makes my heart yearn for "home." I considered it a privilege to entertain them for dinner. As they kept a *glat kosher* life style I bought several new place settings for the occasion, knowing that they wouldn't eat from plates or silverware that might have touched both milk and meat. I went to the kosher butcher and bought the best chicken that God had ever made and cooked it to perfection, with side dishes and dessert worthy of a Prime Minister. Since I had a luncheon to attend that same day I had prepared everything ahead of time. The food only needed reheating and the salad to be tossed. Just as I was beaming over my table, surely set for royalty, my husband called and said, "They cancelled. They can't come."

I was immensely disappointed at first, but then brightened. "Lord, you knew this would happen, so I'm going to leave everything where it is and see why you had me prepare such a feast." And off I went to my luncheon.

It was a Christian women's luncheon to which my mother, my mother-in-law and my niece Karen, the daughter of my husband's sister, were also coming. I was so pleased that they were joining me as my two Moms and I had been doing Bible studies every Tuesday for several months. As my own Mom and I talked and as we looked at the Hebrew Scriptures together on Tuesdays she began to see the Jewishness of Jesus and was losing her fear that we were talking about a *goyisha* (gentile) god. We went over many of the 300 Messianic prophesies of the Messiah in the *Tenach* (the Old Testament or Covenant), though we surely didn't get to them all. We studied the many Old Covenant prophesies about the Messiah, where and to whom he would be born, what his character would be like, how we were to regard him, that he would be the son of God, how he would die, even how he would be buried. With each prophesy we would look at the New Covenant to see how Yeshua fulfilled every one of them. Though neither one of them ever came to the point of accepting him as their own personal Messiah both Moms enjoyed the study and learning more about their own Jewish Scriptures than they'd ever known before.

"No one could master-mind a plan to fulfill all those hundreds of years of predications, especially one's own death," I pointed out. They agreed. "Would you like to invite him into your own lives now?" I would ask them. My Mom would say over and over, "I'm not ready." My mother-in-law would respond with a resolute shrug and say something I never understood about it not being her time. Yet both were always happy to meet again the following week.

Now here we were together at this luncheon. After a lunch that was not nearly as good as the dinner that I had planned for that night, we sang some worship songs together and then the speaker, whose name was April Lupien shared her "testimony," the remarkable story of how she had come to know the Lord and what wonderful things He had done in her life since. Both moms had heard a number similar testimonies on TV and on the several tapes to which they had listened. It was my hope that these testimonies would touch their hearts and draw them to him so that they too would know the same acceptance and love of God that I had come to know through Yeshua.

After April told her story, she then said that she would like to pray for anyone who had a need for healing in their bodies. My mom had suffered from severe migraine headaches for many years, so I asked her if she wanted to go for prayer. "Well, it's worth a try, I guess," she answered. This was not exactly a declaration of faith, but we went for prayer anyway. April took Mom's hand, smiling at her she had asked her what she needed prayer for. "Headaches. For years," Mom said wincing like she had one now, which she didn't. April then asked her if she knew the Lord. "I've never really accepted Him but I know who He is," she said. April asked her if she'd like to accept him now. To my great surprise and delight Mom simply said, "Yes, I would. It's time." She bowed her head, opened her heart to Yeshua and prayed with April, asking Him to forgive her for her sins and to come into her heart and be Lord of her life from now on.

She lifted her head and gave me with the brightest smile, such as I had not seen on her face since I had my last baby. "I did it," she said. "I accepted the Lord." She seemed as pleased about it as I was. My own heart overflowed with joy. "Mom, now I know why the Lord had me prepare a feast. It's a celebration of your coming to Him! We'll call Dad and tell him to come for dinner."

My mother-in-law, Sylvia, had left the luncheon early to take Karen home so she had not been there when Mom went for prayer. Thinking that she may have been able to get back in time for the end of the meeting, she returned. We met her in the parking lot as we were leaving. My mom said excitedly, "Syl, I accepted the Lord." The expression on my mother-in-law's face turned to a frown as she said, "I'm so jealous."

How about that, I thought. "You could accept him too right now," I suggested hopefully. Pausing for a moment, she then answered almost sadly, "No, it doesn't seem to be my time." I wondered what would seem to be her time.

"Well, come for dinner at my house. We're having a celebration." She was happy to come. We invited another friend and I called my Dad and told him to take the train and that I would pick him up at the station. "Don't tell Dad anything. I want to tell him," Mom said. It was hard to act like business as usual when he got into my car, as I was overflowing with excitement. Having someone you love come to the Lord is like that person having the same disease that you once had but found the cure for, and now they had found it, too. I knew he would be as excited as I was for basically the same reason. We both wanted so much for Mom to share with us the security of having God in our lives.

We returned from the train station and came through the back door. Mom who had stayed with my kids while I picked Dad up, immediately greeted him in the kitchen. Smiling expectantly, her face glowing, Mom asked him, "Do I look any different?" He looked her up and down, checking to see if it was a new dress or a new haircut. Then a knowing smile spread across his face. He turned around to set his umbrella in a corner, then, turning again to her, he opened his arms wide and said, "You have Yeshua in your heart, I can see it in your eyes!" He wrapped his arms around her and lifting her off the ground he spun her around, something I had never seen them do before.

My husband was late for dinner, and had called to tell us to start without him. We were all seated around the dinner table when he got there and he proceeded to go around the table, shaking hands with the men and kissing the women and children. When he got to my mom he pulled back and looked into her eyes for a moment and then said, "Oh no, not you too." He knew! He could tell – he apparently recognized that light in her eyes too.

Within a few days Mom told me that she had felt as if

she'd been carrying a heavy burden on her shoulders, like a back-pack, but when she asked the Lord to forgive her for her sins, the burden was lifted off of her and she felt lighter than ever. She hadn't even realized that she was carrying it until it was no longer there but she now knew that she'd been carrying it for many years. I wasn't sure exactly just what sins my mom had committed, but I knew enough from my own experience to know that we all carry a great weight of shame and failure somewhere in our damaged lives. I knew that unresolved hurt leads to some measure of bitterness in our hearts, even if we try to ignore it or to hide it. I knew we all have been victimized by the Fall and the "chaos" this life often brings. And I knew that made even my own mother a candidate for the release that repentance brings. Mom now belonged to the Lord too.

As I write this, it is over twenty-five years later and Mom has continued to rely on the Lord, drawing great strength and peace from Him. "He's in charge," she continually reminds us, trusting in His providence in her life and ours. Her faithful prayers no doubt gird us up in many an instance, I'm sure. Oh, and by the way, Mom no longer has migraine headaches.

Chapter 12

I continued to meet with both moms for the Tuesday morning Bible study, though now my own Mom had more to contribute as the Lord was teaching her things of Himself now that His Spirit dwelt within her. It was fascinating to watch her grow. The Bible tells us that "the things of the spirit are foolishness to the natural man," that is, the person without the spirit of God. Suddenly, what didn't make sense to her intellect just weeks before, she now began to grasp spiritually. You can learn things *about* Yeshua from the Bible but only through revelation, which is imparted by the Spirit of the Lord, can you begin to know Him personally and develop a relationship with Him. The spiritual part of her had come alive now that she had accepted Yeshua's atonement. My mother-in-law, Sylvia, however, continued to report, "It just doesn't seem to be my time." What in the world would be her time, I wondered again.

On *Yom Kippur* the Lord spoke to me and said, "Take your mother-in-law for lunch at the mall." Surely I must not have heard that correctly. Would God tell me to have lunch on *Yom Kippur*, the day of fasting? And at the mall, on the holiest day of the year? If he'd told me to take her to Synagogue, that would have sounded like God to me. I knew His voice, however, and though the words had seemed unlike anything I would expect from God, I obeyed and called her and invited her to go to the mall with me for lunch. It turned out, though it was *Yom Kippur*, relatively non-observant that she was, she was already going to the mall with my sister-in-law Terri who was also a believer, though not Jewish. I told her I'd pick them up in an hour.

We talked as usual through lunch, including about the Lord and the Bible. Then, as we got into the car after lunch, I asked her what I had not thought to ask her before. "Mom, since you say you know that Yeshua is the Messiah, what keeps you from accepting him into your own life as Lord?"

"Why, I'm waiting for my testimony to happen," she exclaimed. Well, now I understood what she was waiting for when she said, "My time isn't yet." She had heard so many "testimonies" of people going through such miraculous things where God had profoundly met them that she was waiting for something miraculous to happen to her.

"Mom," I began to explain, "those things happen to some people and they are wonderful, but it isn't required to have such dramatic things happen to you. That's why those folks are on TV or speaking at luncheons, because it's so special. It's just as special, maybe even more so, for you as a Jewish woman to realize who the Messiah is and open your heart to him. You don't have to wait for something to happen. You can receive him right now, right here, or anywhere."

She clapped her hands. "Oh I didn't know that. All right, lets do it now," she said and without hesitation, she reached for my hands, bowed her head and began praying like she'd been doing it for years: "Yeshua, I'm sorry I took so long. I do know You died to pay for my sins and that You fulfilled all those prophesies in my Jewish Bible. I thank you, Lord, that You've forgiven all those wrong things I did. Now please come and live in my heart and help me to live the way You want me to. I accept you as Lord of my life. Amen."

"Amen," Terri and I echoed. So right there in the mall

parking lot, on *Yom Kippur*, my Jewish mother-in-law Sylvia opened her heart and let God come in and soothe away burdens she too had carried for many years. The change in her from that moment on was dramatic, maybe not to everyone else as she never told her sisters or her children about her faith in Yeshua. But to me, who knew what changes were happening in her life, I knew how much she attempted to line her life up with what she read in her Bible in order to live a righteous life before God.

Within a few years, after many struggles in our marriage, beginning way before I became a Believer, my husband and I were divorced. It was not my preference. The Lord proved to me then and has many times since, that He is indeed "a very present help in trouble." A powerful sense of His presence carried me through. Had I not known the forgiveness of the Lord and His loving acceptance, I doubt I would have been able to forgive others as He enabled me to do. I learned that forgiveness, both receiving it and giving it, is what enables us to be free of the crippling effects of bitterness, heartbreak, and failure, sometimes on an ongoing basis as new incidents and new pains came up. My children's pain, as a result of the divorce, was especially difficult to navigate and I tried to teach them too to forgive. I have come to trust that what I commit to God and truly trust Him for, He will take care of, including me and my children.

I never thought of Sylvia as my "ex" mother-in-law. Though we were not in each other's lives as we had been, we continued to love each other and see each other periodically. When she developed cancer and needed much care, she was moved into my now ex-husband's house in order for her to be cared for by him.

Once when she was in the hospital for tests she called me and asked if I would come see her. Of course. I hadn't seen her since she'd been sick and I wasn't prepared for how the medication had affected her. Entering her hospital room I was shocked to see her so changed. I hardly recognized the moon shaped face before me as she lay on the hospital bed. She had always been meticulous and small in stature, now she was large and swollen. I might have thought I was in the wrong room had I not heard her voice calling me by my name. She greeting me with such affection as I leaned over to kiss her hello, though I felt as if I was going to faint from the shock. "Look at her hands," the Lord said inside me. As I did I was comforted by the same hands I knew to be hers, even then, perfectly manicured. Somehow her hands seemed untouched by the disease. I thanked the Lord silently for his assistance in strengthening me.

We began to talk as we always did. "He's never let me feel pain," she told me with a smile. "I wanted to put a sign over my bed telling everyone how Jesus has taken care of me, even in this." She had never discussed the Lord with anyone in her family but Karen, who had come to know the Lord in a sweet and special way herself, and had married a Catholic. Mom told me that she had asked Karen to have a priest come to baptize her and so Karen had brought her priest and Mom was baptized in her hospital room. It was obviously very meaningful to her. I was glad she had Karen to share the Lord with.

We talked for a while as two women who love each other, about the children we both loved. Knowing that her life would soon be over, she said she had no fear of death and that she was assured she would soon be with Yeshua and was looking forward to seeing Him face to face. Her peace was evident. When I knew she grew tired, I kissed her again, and looking into her eyes I knew this was likely the last time we would see each other till we were both in heaven. I then left my dear mother-in-law Sylvia saying a silent farewell.

Two months later I received an unexpected phone call from my (ex) sister-in-law, Barbara. "Mom is not expected to last throughout the night. If you'd like to see her you'd better come now." I was grateful for her call and prayed all the way to the nursing home that I would be able to get there before she died. I so wanted to be with her as she departed into the arms of Yeshua, to whisper to her that he would be waiting for her. As I drove through the dark night as quickly as I could, I heard the familiar voice of the Lord say, "She's with me." Yet doubt immediately rose up inside of me. I wanted so much to see her before she died. "She'll still be here when I get there," I assured myself. I glanced at the clock on the dash board for some reason. I arrived at the nursing home exactly five minutes later. Barbara was standing on the steps outside the building when I pulled up. She looked at me through her tears and said quietly, "Mom died five minutes ago."

I walked into the room where her body lay on the bed, tucked under crisp white sheets, dressed in a white hospital gown. Her children were crying around her, including my ex-husband and a brother and sister-in-law I hadn't seen for years. We hugged each other with the sad warmth that comes at such times, and I walked to her bedside. Such grief pervaded the room. There was nothing in the room that spoke of the lovely things she treasured having around her, she wore no pretty and feminine nightgown, there was nothing that spoke of her ways. She lay so still. I took one of her lovely hands in my own and looked into her peaceful face.

While the sound of her children's grieving was all

around me, a joy welled up inside me. I was the only one in the room who knew where she now was. "She's with him! She's with the Lord!" I kept telling myself at the wonder of it. In a way that I had long ago come to recognize as the Lord reminding me of a Scripture verse, "To be absent from the body is to be present with the Lord," went through my mind. I knew that the real her, her spirit, was now in heaven because she had opened her heart to Yeshua on that *Yom Kippor* day, and lived her life with him ever since. While all the others wept with sadness I also wept, but with such a humble gratefulness to God that she was now experiencing the unhindered and inexpressible joy that he had once revealed to me is the atmosphere of heaven.

As I was about to leave, my eyes caught sight of something familiar on her night table. It was the one thing of hers that was in the room. On the night table stood a tiny ceramic "Christmas" tree I had made for her a number of years before. It was simply an evergreen, about 3 inches high, symbolizing the birth of Messiah but without all the decorations. It was to mean Yeshua only, and none of what Christmas has come to represent that is so unlike Him. The little tree was the only thing she'd taken with her to the nursing home, the only thing that meant enough to her that she had kept it with her. Perhaps it was her way of staying connected with the Lord – or with me. In the end, it was the only thing that said who she really was, a Believer in Yeshua, though no one in the room knew it but me. I quietly slipped it into my pocket. It sits on my desk now as I write, reminding me that she's with Him, and one day we'll be together again.

Section 4

Ellen and Gili

Chapter 13

I was in Israel again. I had been there several times since that first life changing trip. One of those times had been for my daughter Ellen's wedding. The time before that was to become more acquainted with Tamir, the young Israeli soldier, also a Believer, whom she had met on a trip to Israel with my mother and brother and our Messianic Synagogue. Shortly thereafter she transferred from her college in Philadelphia to Tel Aviv University.

When Ellen left for Israel, as I watched her drive away from me and I felt the piercing longing for my daughter already welling up inside, the Lord spoke to me and said, "I will give you My peace if you will take it." "I'll take it, Lord," I replied and never once did I fear for her safety and well being and though I missed her a very great deal, I had peace about her being there. Before the semester was over they were engaged.

Fourteen months after the wedding in Tel Aviv, my other daughter Jenny and I flew to Israel for the birth of my first grandchild. It was the hottest summer the Middle East had had in forty years as we awaited the arrival of this baby. Finally, she was born, a beautiful little girl whom they named Gili, which in Hebrew means "Rejoice." Rejoice I did with her arrival. A little red-head, she was more than just my granddaughter. To me she represented God's faithfulness to His promises to Israel, to the Jewish people.

If the Jewish historian, Max Dimont is correct that the Jews who lived in Eastern Europe were those who had come out of Judea in 586 BCE when the Babylonians captured Jerusalem and deported it's citizens to Babylon, since all four of my grandparents had come from Russia to the United States, then Gili was the first on both sides of my family to be born in the Promised Land in 2,574 years! Her birth was a testimony to God's sovereign power to keep His promise to give the Land of Israel to the physical descendents of Abraham.

No amount of warfare, persecution or even genocide had been able to cause the extinction of the Jewish people. We remain, by God's sovereign keeping. But even more worthy of rejoicing, in fulfillment of the greatest promise of all, we in our family are a fulfillment of the desire of the heart of the God of Abraham, Isaac and Jacob that He would be our God and we would be His people.

"Thus says the Lord, who gives the sun for light by day, and the fixed order of the moon and the stars for light by night, who stirs up the seas so that its waves roar; the Lord of hosts is His name: If this fixed order departs from before Me, declares the Lord, then the offspring of Israel also shall cease from being a nation before Me forever. Thus says the Lord, If the heavens above can be measured, and the foundations of the earth searched out below, then I will also cast off all the offspring of Israel... declares the Lord."

"Behold the days are coming," declares the Lord. This is the covenant which I will make with the house of Israel...declares the Lord, "I will put my law within them, and on their heart I will write it; and I will be their God, and they will be My people." (Jer. 31:33, 35-37)

<<>>

Prayer of Connection With God

*I*f **this book has touched your heart** so that you too wish to know Messiah Yeshua as we in our family have come to know Him, a simple prayer of repentance will bridge the gap between you and God. Yeshua said, "No one comes to the Father except through Me." I have found that to be true. If that is the desire of your heart, you may want to pray the prayer below.

It would be best to tell God where you know you have sinned. It is always best to be open and truthful with God. He knows anyway but longs for you to tell Him your most intimate thoughts, to share all of your life with Him. If you are like I was initially and aren't sure what separates you from the Lord, ask Him to show you and expect that He will. It may not be today but He will lovingly show it to you.

The whole purpose of His coming was to bring forgiveness of the sin that separates us from God. We become His when we realize our need for His atoning death in order to be acceptable to God. Let's pray:

God of Abraham, Isaac and Jacob, I accept that Yeshua (Jesus) is the Son of God and the promised Messiah and that

He took the punishment that my sins deserve. Please forgive me for _____. (Tell God of your sins or ask Him to show you what He's offering forgiveness to you for, so you can repent for it.)

I ask you to forgive me for living so independently from You and I now ask You to be Lord of my life. Please teach me how to live in a manner worthy of You. I thank you that because of Yeshua's death I am now restored to God. Please fill me with Your Holy Spirit and help me to walk in Your ways. I want you to be my God, and I want to be your son (or daughter). In Yeshua's Name, Amen.

If you have prayed that prayer and meant it from your heart, God heard you and took you seriously. He will respond to you! Tell someone! If you are truly His, you will want to share your good news with others

If you are Jewish and you are not sure about Yeshua (Jesus) being the Jewish Messiah, may I suggest you pray the following prayer:

God of Abraham, Isaac and Jacob, I want to know You as my God and I want to be Yours. I want to know what it is to have a personal relationship with You, Lord. I have been told in this book that Yeshua (Jesus) is the only way to that relationship. If He really the Messiah and Your Son, please show me. I want to know the truth. Please teach me how to live so as to be pleasing to you. Thank you. Amen.

I would be pleased to have you send me an email and let me know of your prayer. I will be glad to answer your email.

You may contact Lonnie Lane at
MessiahsHope@aol.com
or
904-382-8523

Printed in the United States
63713LVS00002B/286-645